Fiorello's Sister

Religion, Theology, and the Holocaust
Steven T. Katz, *Series Editor*

Studio portrait of Gemma La Guardia in St. Louis, circa
1898. *Courtesy of the LaGuardia and Wagner Archives.*

Fiorello's Sister

Gemma La Guardia Gluck's Story

Gemma La Guardia Gluck

NEWLY EXPANDED EDITION

EDITED BY ROCHELLE G. SAIDEL

Incorporating My Story *by Gemma La Guardia Gluck*

Syracuse University Press

Syracuse University Press, Syracuse, New York 13244–5160

First Edition 2007

07 08 09 10 11 12   6 5 4 3 2

Includes the original text of *My Story,* by Gemma La Guardia Gluck,
edited by S. L. Shneiderman (New York: David McKay, 1961).

This book is supported in part by a grant from Remember the Women Institute.

The paper used in this publication meets the minimum requirements of American
National Standard for Information Sciences—Permanence of Paper for Printed
Library Materials, ANSI Z39.48–1984.∞™

For a listing of books published and distributed by Syracuse University Press,
visit our Web site at SyracuseUniversityPress.syr.edu.

ISBN-13: 978-0-8156-0861-5   ISBN-10: 0-8156-0861-6

Library of Congress Cataloging-in-Publication Data

Gluck, Gemma La Guardia, 1881–1962.
Fiorello's sister : Gemma La Guardia Gluck's story / Gemma La Guardia Gluck ;
edited by Rochelle G. Saidel.—Newly expanded ed.; 1st ed.
p. cm.—(Religion, theology, and the Holocaust)
"Incorporating My story by Gemma La Guardia Gluck."
Includes bibliographical references.
ISBN-13: 978–0-8156-0861-5 (pbk. : alk. paper)
ISBN-10: 0–8156-0861-6 (pbk. : alk. paper)
1. Gluck, Gemma La Guardia, 1881–1962. 2. Ravensbrück (Concentration camp) 3.
World War, 1939–1945—Prisoners and prisons, German. 4. World War,
1939–1945—Personal narratives, American. 5. Concentration camp inmates—
Germany—Ravensbrück—Biography. 6. Political prisoners—Germany—Biography.
I. Saidel, Rochelle G. II. Gluck, Gemma La Guardia, 1881–1962. My story. III.
Title.
D805.5.R38G58 2007
940.53'161—dc22
[B]   2006102112

Manufactured in the United States of America

This memoir is dedicated to the martyred women of Ravensbrück, the thousands who perished and the few who survived. Their valiant resistance to the Nazis preserved the image of human dignity in a time of inhuman brutality.

—Gemma La Guardia Gluck, 1961

This new edition of *My Story,* now entitled *Fiorello's Sister: Gemma La Guardia Gluck's Story,* is dedicated to the memory of Gemma La Guardia Gluck, a brave, resilient, and optimistic woman; and to the memory of S. L. Shneiderman, a talented and prolific writer and editor.

—Rochelle G. Saidel, 2007

Rochelle G. Saidel is founder and director of Remember the Women Institute, based in New York City, which carries out academic research and cultural projects that integrate women into history. She is the author of *The Jewish Women of Ravensbrück Concentration Camp*, a finalist for the 2004 National Jewish Book Awards in both the Holocaust Studies and Women's Studies categories. She is also the author of *Never Too Late to Remember: The Politics Behind New York City's Holocaust Museum* and *The Outraged Conscience: Seekers of Justice for Nazi War Criminals in America*. She served as curator of an art and history exhibit on Ravensbrück for the Florida Holocaust Museum and is a consultant for other projects related to that women's concentration camp. Dr. Saidel received her Ph.D. in political science from the Graduate School and University Center of City University of New York. She was a research fellow at the Yad Vashem International Institute for Holocaust Research in fall 2006 and is also a senior researcher at the Center for the Study of Women and Gender, University of São Paulo, Brazil. A citizen of Israel and the United States, she divides her time among Jerusalem, New York, and São Paulo.

Contents

Illustrations

Preface to the Original Edition

THE NAZI HOLOCAUST with its unprecedented crimes
against humanity will long remain an unresolved paradox for
historians, sociologists, and psychologists to ponder. For the
horrors of Nazism were not brought on Europe by barbarian
hordes but by a civilized nation that had achieved the summits
of art and science.

Perhaps the seeds of this cataclysm can be found in the
teachings of Friedrich Nietzsche, the great nineteenth-century
German philosopher who prophesied a second deluge. He
foresaw the collapse of the values which for centuries had nur-
tured Western civilization and the emergence of a superman,
whose irrational will to power *(Der Wille zur Macht)* would
lead him to victory over the whole human species. Adolf
Hitler, a fervent disciple of Nietzsche, saw himself as the em-
bodiment of that superman, destined to unleash the elemental
forces that slumbered in the German "master race."

The vast literature dealing with the Nazi era and its terrible
degradation of human dignity has not penetrated to the core of
the paradox. Numerous personal accounts and extensive documentation have revealed the tremendous scope of the genocide
so methodically organized by the Nazi machine and carried
out by its specialized operational groups. The diaries of the vic-

tims, often published posthumously, and the memoirs written by survivors cry out to us in their accounts of almost unbelievable personal suffering. A few of them also record some aspects of the strange way of life that went on in the infamous concentration camps.[1]

What really happens to the individual and his relationships to his fellow men under such circumstances?[2] For an answer to this question, we must await a work of genius still unwritten. Attempts made thus far seem to have fallen short. Some of the novels already published distort the tragic events they purport to explain, or reveal their authors' misconceptions.

Time is needed to put the Nazi era in its proper perspective, time that will calm the passions that becloud the issues and obscure the real characters of both the torturers and their victims. In the case of the American Civil War, nearly a century passed before literature—in works of fiction and history—could give us a true appraisal of that time of tragedy.

My Story was written with no intention of carrying a message, but the message is there, immanent in every line. It is heartening to see the solidarity and readiness for self-sacrifice shown by so many of the camp's inmates. The International Table Gemma La Guardia Gluck organized is symbolic. Here she brought together women from many nations that the Nazis were trying to incite against one another.

1. Since 1961 there has been a significant number of memoirs that record women's experiences in concentration camps. [RGS]

2. Although this is a woman's memoir, both Gluck and Shneiderman use male-gendered language, as was common in 1961. In order to maintain the flavor of the memoir, I have not changed their original language. [RGS]

The affection that the women of Ravensbrück cherished for Mrs. Gluck, their teacher in clandestine English classes, is recorded in the little album they gave her on the last Christmas before liberation. The entries in a multitude of languages, especially those written by the Polish women used as "rabbits" in the Nazis' cruel "medical experiments," bear witness to the courageous struggle of these women to keep the human spirit alive in the abyss of death and humiliation.[3]

Gemma La Guardia Gluck was seized by the Gestapo late in World War II when the Nazi tide had already receded from its crest. The last chapter of the "Final Solution of the Jewish Problem," a term the Nazis coined for the liquidation of eleven million Jews in Europe, was being written. In the spring of 1944 the chief architect of the "solution," Adolf Eichmann, appeared in Budapest with a blueprint for the annihilation of almost eight hundred thousand Hungarian Jews, who had not been physically harmed up to that time. It was in his dealings with Hungarian Jewry that Eichmann revealed his identity as the master mind of the "final solution."

In managing the death factories, Adolf Eichmann took extreme precautions not to leave evidence of his direct involvement in the crimes. Only in exceptional instances did he concern himself with individuals. Such cases were those of rel-

---

3. The term *rabbits,* from *lapins* in French, has the same meaning as *guinea pigs* in English. This refers to seventy-four Polish Christian political prisoners who were used as human guinea pigs in horrific experiments on their legs in Ravensbrück concentration camp. The Nazis used these women to simulate the wounds of soldiers in battlefield conditions. See chapter 12 for more information. [RGS]

atives of leaders in the Allied world. These were either sent to extermination camps in revenge for the anti-Nazi activities of their kin, or held hostages for possible exchange for important Germans.[4] This was the case with Mrs. Gemma Gluck.

Eichmann's order to arrest Mrs. Gluck undoubtedly was an act of retaliation for the anti-Nazi activities of her brother. The sequence of events proves it. On April 19, 1944, Mayor Fiorello La Guardia appeared on the steps of New York's City Hall before a mass demonstration of Polish Jews commemorating the first anniversary of the uprising of the Warsaw ghetto. La Guardia warned the Nazis that they would pay for their crimes, and predicted the imminent downfall of the Hitler regime.

Less than one month later, on May 12, 1944, Hungarian detectives, accompanied by Nazi S.S. officers, came to the house in Budapest where Gemma, older sister of Fiorello La Guardia, had been living for many years with her Jewish husband, Herman Gluck. They searched for a shortwave radio with which she might be in contact with her brother. On June 7, Gemma and Herman Gluck were arrested. After several days in a Budapest prison they were sent to the Mauthausen extermination camp. Shortly afterward Gemma La Guardia Gluck was shipped to the women's camp at Ravensbrück, where she was placed in a special section for members of prominent families.

Among the numerous documents that the attorney general of the State of Israel submitted at Eichmann's trial was a Nazi Foreign Office memorandum written by its expert on Jewish

4. Other political hostages in the camp included the niece of Charles de Gaulle. See Anthonioz (1999). [RGS]

affairs, Eberhardt von Thadden, who was in charge of Section "Inland II." Von Thadden was mentioned frequently during the Eichmann trial in Jerusalem. His personal testimony had to be taken in Germany because Israeli authorities felt he was too deeply involved in Nazi crimes to be granted the immunity from prosecution that would allow him to enter Israel.

In his memorandum Eberhardt von Thadden reported on his efforts to persuade Eichmann not to send Gemma La Guardia Gluck to an extermination camp, but to hold her as a hostage instead. Addressed to the German Legation in Budapest, this document reads:

> In a conversation held in Budapest on the 23d of May, 1944, between the undersigned and the S.S. Obersturmbannführer Eichmann, the latter stated that he had ordered the arrest of Frau Gluck, a Jewess, sister of the Mayor of New York, Fiorello La Guardia, if such arrest had not already been carried out. It has been requested that, because of the position of her brother, Frau Gluck not be sent with a mass transport to the Eastern territories, but rather be held in a special camp in the Reich or in Hungary in order to be available for eventual political use.
>
> von Thadden [5]

5. Two documents referring to Gemma were presented at the Eichmann trial in Jerusalem in 1961. This letter from von Thadden to the Foreign Office, dated June 6, 1944, is trial document no. 516. Trial document no. 1020, dated July 14, 1944, originates from Eichmann's Section, IVA4b. Someone named Vansinger writes to von Thadden to advise him that Gemma is racially of first-degree mixed origin and therefore considered a

During a visit I made to Israel shortly before the Eichmann trial, my attention was drawn to this unusual document. It was shown to me by Professor Marjan Muszkat, legal adviser of Yad Vashem, the research center where all the documentation for the prosecution of Adolf Eichmann was prepared. At that time Professor Muszkat was under the impression that Mrs. Gluck had perished in the Nazi death camps.

However, on returning to New York I contacted the widow of the late mayor, Marie La Guardia, and learned from her that Mrs. Gluck was alive and would soon reach her eightieth birthday. Mrs. Gluck was living with her daughter in a small apartment in a municipal housing project that was built during Fiorello La Guardia's administration as mayor of New York. I went to see her. Although she had been partially paralyzed by a stroke, her manner of speaking, her energetic gestures, the flash of her dark eyes, and her horn-rimmed spectacles were very reminiscent of her dynamic brother Fiorello.

It was a shock to Gemma La Guardia Gluck to learn that she had been a hostage to Adolf Eichmann.

Soon after her return to the United States Mrs. Gluck had written a memoir. It began with a family chronicle, telling of her childhood with Fiorello in New York and in Arizona at the turn of the century; described her happy years as a young woman in cosmopolitan Budapest, and gave an account of her tragic experiences in the concentration camps. Mrs. Gluck may well have been the only native American woman sent by

_____

Jewess. Because she is the sister of the mayor of New York City, on instructions of the Reichsführer-SS (Himmler), she is being kept as a political hostage in Ravensbrück concentration camp (YV). [RGS]

the Nazis to the camps.[6] *My Story* is an expansion of that memoir.

It is a story of the unconquerable human soul. Unpretentious, sincere, moving, it throbs with warmth, with kindness, and, astonishingly, with hope.

S. L. Shneiderman, 1961

6. There were other American women at the camp. For example, according to Póltawska (1964, 136), Aka Kolodziejczak, a Polish woman who was an American citizen, was released from the camp in December 1943. She gives no further details. Rossiter (1986, 204–10) mentions a native-born American at Ravensbrück named Virginia D'Albert Lake. She had married a French aristocrat and joined the resistance with him. She was sent to Torgau subcamp, and in February 1945 her mother convinced Secretary of State Cordell Hull to have her transferred to a Red Cross camp at Lake Constance. [RGS]

Acknowledgments

I AM GRATEFUL to the individuals and institutions that helped to make *Fiorello's Sister: Gemma La Guardia Gluck's Story* a reality. Gemma's grandchildren, Gladys Roberts McMilleon and Richard Denes, as well as other members of the La Guardia family, provided input and encouraged me. I am especially thankful to Gladys, who became my friend as this project progressed. Her middle name is Gemma, and her personality reflects her grandmother's generous and loving spirit. S. L. Shneiderman's late wife Eileen Shneiderman, his son Ben Shneiderman, and daughter Helen Shneiderman Sarid were supportive regarding my republishing the work that he edited in 1961. Ben Shneiderman and Richard Denes, rights holders of the 1961 edition of Gemma's memoir, *My Story,* graciously granted me the rights to edit and issue this new edition. The Five Millers Family Foundation funded research, and the Fiorello H. La Guardia Foundation provided a generous publication grant.

Archival work was carried out at the S. L. Shneiderman Archives housed at the Diaspora Research Institute, Tel Aviv University; the Wagner and LaGuardia Archives at LaGuardia Community College, City University of New York (with thanks to Maureen Drennan); Yad Vashem in Jerusalem; the

Israel State Archive; Mahn- und Gedenkstätte Ravensbrück; and the Leo Baeck Institute Archive, Center for Jewish History in New York. Information from Michael Skakun led me to the file at the Leo Baeck Institute. Dail Stolow helped me locate Gemma's relatives, and the The Jewish Community of Trieste provided early family documentation.

My research was carried out under the auspices of Remember the Women Institute, where some members of the advisory board, especially Sonja Hedgepeth and Elizabeth Howitt, made sound suggestions during various phases. The professional input of my son Daniel Wolk, a computer expert, and my daughter Esther Wolk, a librarian, as well as sage advice from my husband Guilherme Ary Plonski, were gratifying.

The enthusiastic interest of Natalia Indrimi, director of the Centro Primo Levi for Italian Jewish Studies of the Center for Jewish History, led to my finding archival material in the very building in which she works, and Centro Primo Levi is cooperating in the postpublication phase of this book. Ellen Goodman, acquisitions editor of Syracuse University Press, believed in this book and brought it to fruition, along with the Editorial Department and copyeditor Linda Cuckovich.

Most of all, although I never met them, I thank Gemma La Guardia Gluck, who recorded her remarkable memoir, and S. L. Shneiderman, who skillfully edited it in 1961.

Rochelle G. Saidel, 2007

Fiorello's Sister

Prologue

"EVEN SERIOUS SCHOLARSHIP needs a little luck," as Helen Shneiderman Sarid wrote to me. She was referring to the series of coincidences and the remarkable good fortune that led me to the typed manuscript and page proofs for Gemma La Guardia Gluck's *My Story,* edited in 1961 by S. L. Shneiderman, Helen's father. I found them in a most unlikely archive: the Leo Baeck Institute at the Center for Jewish History in New York.

I had discovered Gemma's published memoir after 1980, when my interest in Ravensbrück concentration camp began. I found a copy in the U.S. Holocaust Memorial Museum library, then purchased my own from a dealer of out-of-print and rare books. An abridged account of Gemma's time in Ravensbrück became a chapter of my 2004 book, *The Jewish Women of Ravensbrück Concentration Camp.* However, I decided that her entire story should be shared with new generations of readers and began searching archives to bring *My Story* up to date. I investigated all of the appropriate places, especially the New York City Municipal Archives, the LaGuardia and Wagner Archives at LaGuardia Community College, the S. L. Shneiderman Archives at the Diaspora Research Institute, Tel Aviv University, and Yad Vashem. Gemma's and Shneiderman's family members also gave me leads, material, and encouragement.

I thought I had all of my bases covered, and then, soon before this book was completed, I was told about the existence of the 1961 page proofs and manuscript. There is no information in the Leo Baeck Institute archive about when this material was deposited, or by whom. Shneiderman must have been the source, but why would these papers have been placed in an archive that specializes in German Jewry? The only extremely remote connection is that Gemma wrote in her memoir about Gertrud Luckner, stating that she had helped Rabbi Leo Baeck. The microfilm of the documents related to *My Story* is at the end of a number of German memoirs, and I was first told by an archivist that Gemma's memoir was in German. I am extremely lucky that I happened upon them.

The story of the discovery of the manuscript and page proofs began in April 2006, when Natalia Indrimi, director of the Centro Primo Levi for Italian Jewish Studies at the Center for Jewish History in New York, invited me to meet her at the center. She had learned about my work on Ravensbrück and Gemma and wanted to talk with me about it. She expressed her interest in my plans to republish Gemma's memoir, and we agreed to stay in touch. A few weeks later, she invited me to an unrelated program she had organized at the Center for Jewish History.

I attended, and in this building that houses the Leo Baeck Institute I met an acquaintance, author and researcher Michael Skakun. He told me that he was working in all of the archives of the center, compiling a bibliography on the Holocaust. "There is even something on your subject," he said. "Ravensbrück?" I asked. "No," he answered. "Gemma La Guardia Gluck." I was astounded.

The Center for Jewish History is a consortium that includes the Leo Baeck Institute, YIVO Institute for Jewish Research, the American Jewish Historical Society, the American Sephardi Federation, and Yeshiva University Museum. None of these institutions seemed a likely archival source for material on Gemma, and I never had reason to check them. Michael could not remember in which institution's archive he had seen the material, and the archives were by then closed for the night. My educated guess was the American Jewish Historical Society because Gemma was born and died a citizen of the United States, and her brother played a significant role in American history. A second idea was that Shneiderman, as a Yiddish writer, may have chosen to deposit his manuscript with YIVO. I was wrong.

By the end of the next day I had established that there was a file folder, as well as microfilm, in the Leo Baeck Institute, and the day afterward I was reviewing this unexpected treasure. I found a typed manuscript with handwritten corrections and two sets of page proofs. Gemma's original memoir, now apparently lost, was handwritten. As she was partially paralyzed from a stroke before 1961, it is more than likely that Shneiderman either typed this manuscript or had it typed. This accidental find allowed me to restore chapter titles, annotate some information that had been deleted from the 1961 book, and better understand some details. Most of all, it gave me a closer connection to Gemma's story, Shneiderman's editing style, and the original memoir.

Gemma La Guardia Gluck was not as famous as her brother

Fiorello, the beloved mayor of New York City from 1934 to 1945, but her own story is as powerful and as moving as his. Gemma's lifetime spanned from the great wave of immigration to the United States in the 1880s until John F. Kennedy's presidency. By the time she died in New York City in November 1962, she had been a political hostage of the Nazis in Ravensbrück concentration camp and a post-World War II displaced person and refugee. Most of her memoir is a vivid eyewitness account of her ordeal during and immediately after the Holocaust. However, there is much more to Gemma's story. She describes the United States at the end of the nineteenth century and the various places she lived as her U.S. Army bandleader father changed headquarters. She tells of the Native Americans that her mother befriended in Dakota Territory and of how the 1898 sinking of the United States battleship *Maine* in Cuba affected her family.

Gemma's memoir is also a saga of European history from pre-World War I to post-World War II. After her father retired from the army in 1898, when Gemma was seventeen, the family moved to Trieste. Gemma shares with readers her insights concerning her brother Fiorello's ambitions as a young man and how his early position in the United States Consulate in Fiume, then part of Hungary, led him to return to the United States to pursue his education and career.

Gemma and Fiorello's mother was Jewish, and their maternal grandmother was part of the prestigious Italian-Jewish Luzzatto family. Gemma relates how she and her mother stayed in Europe after Fiorello returned to the United States in 1906, and how she married one of her students of English, a Hungarian Jew named Herman Gluck.

Together with Gemma's mother, Herman and Gemma

moved to Budapest, where they had two daughters. Yolanda was born in February 1911, and Irene, seven years later in April 1918. Yolanda remained in Budapest, where she married and had a son, while Irene left for the United States before World War II. Gemma shares with readers details about her beautiful life in Budapest before the arrival of the Nazis and tells us how it dramatically changed for the worse in the spring of 1944.

Gemma's memoir provides valuable information about life and death in Ravensbrück concentration camp from the spring of 1944 until the camp's last days at the end of April 1945. She was sent there by high-level orders because her relationship to Fiorello made her valuable to the Nazis as a political hostage. She was already more than sixty years old when she arrived at the camp, an age that would have meant certain death from starvation, disease, or slave labor for an ordinary prisoner. However, her special status relieved her of the usual regime of harsh slave labor. While she still suffered from the starvation diet and other horrors of the camp, her work assignment was relatively light.

Located about fifty miles from Berlin, Ravensbrück opened as a major concentration camp for women in the spring of 1939. By the time it was liberated by the Soviet Army at the end of April 1945, some 132,000 women from more than forty nations had been imprisoned there, and fewer than 20,000 survived. As Gemma recounts, the categories of prisoners included political prisoners, "asocials," Jehovah's Witnesses, Jews, and criminals, each group with its distinct colored triangle. Political prisoners encompassed members of outlawed political parties such as Communists and Social Democrats, prisoners of war, resistance fighters, and women who had helped to hide Jews. Among those considered "asocial" were Gypsies, lesbians, and prostitutes.

Life in the camp was brutal, and conditions became worse over time, as rations diminished and the population grew. The women were subjected to a long roll call twice a day and back-breaking slave labor. Torture, beatings, dog attacks, and other sadistic practices were routine. Women were even murdered by gassing, first at another location and then inside the camp. Gemma reports the atrocities but also records how some of the women prisoners lifted each other's spirits with small hand-made gifts and other kindnesses. She contributed to this resistance of the spirit by teaching English to the women in her barrack and treating them with motherly kindness.

As the Soviet Army was approaching the camp at the end of April 1945, the Nazis decided it was time to send Gemma to Berlin for a possible hostage exchange. At this time Gemma received the shocking news that her daughter Yolanda and baby grandson Richard had also been incarcerated in Ravensbrück, hidden away in another part of the camp. She, her daughter, and her grandson were liberated from the concentration camp together and brought to Berlin, but their troubles were nowhere near coming to an end.

Berlin was in ruins and the bombs were falling during these last chaotic days before Germany's defeat. Gemma finally managed to find shelter for herself and her family and to contact Fiorello. However, it took two years of struggle and a temporary stay in Denmark before the three could leave Europe for the United States and a reunion with Fiorello. Her famous brother died of cancer soon after her arrival in New York in 1947, and Gemma lived for the rest of her life in a low-income housing project in Queens, New York.

Gemma's original book, *My Story,* could stand alone in telling her personal recollections about a turbulent period of history. She lived in quite a few countries, and some of the cities she lived in belonged to different countries during her lifetime. Her memoir is especially significant as a rare and early firsthand English account of Ravensbrück concentration camp and the travails that survivors faced in the aftermath of the Holocaust. The fact that she is Fiorello La Guardia's sister makes her story all the more fascinating.

However, some aspects of Gemma's saga that were not covered in the original have been addressed here. The text is now illustrated with photographs obtained from archives and members of the La Guardia family. Additional information has been gleaned from documents related to Gemma's arrest by the Nazis. The epilogue for this new edition brings Gemma's story to a conclusion, with information about her memoir's original 1961 publication, her death, and her family. Finally, I have added an appendix consisting of letters between Gemma and Fiorello after her liberation that contain intimate details of her postwar plight.

Gemma was a strong resourceful woman, but she wrote her memoir in a prefeminist world. She does not seem to think that what she accomplished was extraordinary, but the reader can grasp from her modest account that indeed she was capable of taking care of herself and her family during a time when society in Europe and America was more patriarchal than it is today. She knew she was the pawn of forceful men, her arrest and incarceration as a political hostage ordered by Reichsführer Heinrich Himmler and Adolf Eichmann because she was the sister of the powerful anti-Nazi mayor of New York. As she tells readers in her memoir, "I will always say it's much easier for a man to make his destiny than for a girl. It seems to be always somebody else who makes it for her."

While I did not change Gemma's original language, I want to point out to the reader that her terminology is often not the gender-neutral language appropriate for the twenty-first century. When she made reference to events or people that need further explanations today, I added notes with relevant information. I also divided the first and last chapters into two because of their length and subject matter.

Thanks to Gemma La Guardia Gluck's careful recording of her life in her memoir, and to Shneiderman's skillful editing and success in bringing it to print in 1961, we have a significant personal record of Holocaust history, American history, and European history, as well as insights into Gemma and Fiorello's family life. The original edition of *My Story* has been out of print for decades, and it is a privilege to be instrumental in bringing *Fiorello's Sister: Gemma La Guardia Gluck's Story* to new generations of readers.

Rochelle G. Saidel

1

My Childhood with Fiorello

I WAS BORN in an immigrant neighborhood in New York only a few years before the city's harbor became the home of the "Mother of Exiles," that great bronze lady who stands at the gateway to America, holding high the torch of freedom, with the broken shackles of persecution at her feet.

I never dreamed that the true meaning of the Statue of Liberty would be revealed to me more than half a century later when I returned to America as a weary, shattered survivor of the Holocaust the Nazis had unleashed on the lands of Europe. Only then did I see it in the same light as millions of other refugees have seen it.

There were tears in my eyes that day in May 1947, when the vessel, a Liberty ship, bringing me back to America, sailed up the harbor, and I could see the skyline of New York in all its grandeur and magnificence. I was overwhelmed by the thought that my brother Fiorello had been the mayor of this mighty metropolis for twelve years. I remembered with amusement that it had once been my father's fondest dream to make of Fiorello "a second John Philip Sousa."

My father and mother had sailed for America on their wedding day in 1880 and set up their first home in the narrow streets of Greenwich Village in New York. I was their first child, born in New York in the year 1881. Fiorello was born a year later, and my brother Richard was born in the West in 1885.[1]

Achille Luigi Carlo La Guardia came from Foggia near Naples and his bride, Irene Coen, was a native of Trieste. My father was a fine musician, a cornet player, and later became bandmaster in the United States Army.

Our first army post with the 11th Infantry was at Fort Sully, Dakota Territory. I was only a small child in those days, but the wild and woolly West made a vivid impression on my mind. In 1884 there were still many Indians in Dakota.[2] The commanding colonel of Papa's regiment wanted to do him a great favor when he offered to assign a particular house to us. This house stood all by itself on a hill, away from the straight rows of army houses. It was a charming house, but my father feared that Mother, being so young and new in America, would be afraid to be alone when Papa had to be away on duty.

But Mother was all for it, and we moved in. In a few months both my father and the colonel were greatly surprised to see that Mother had become good friends with the Indians who lived nearby the hill. They brought all kinds of gifts, such as handmade blankets, moccasins, beads, and, in turn, she gave them sugar and other staples. The Indians spoke a Spanish dialect, Mother spoke Italian to them, and in this manner they understood each other very well. Mother always said, "No one is so well protected here as I am." And she was right—the Indians loved her and would never have done her any harm.

One night there was a great deal of excitement when a

1. Richard was born when the family was in Fort Sully, Dakota Territory, in 1887.

2. This terminology, rather than Native Americans, was in use in 1961.

prairie fire broke out. An alarm was sounded, and all the women and children were ordered to gather in the hospital. We all had to wrap wet blankets around us. I was about four years old then. All of us children thought the fire was a lot of fun.

Later the 11th Infantry was ordered to Sackett's Harbor, near Watertown, New York. My brothers and I started our elementary school days here. It was the standing procedure at that time for the regiment to move every three years, first to a frontier post and then to a post in a well-settled area. So after three years at Sackett's Harbor we were sent to Fort Huachucha and then to Whipple Barracks near Prescott, Arizona. The six years that we spent in Arizona were the happiest years of our youth.

At that time Prescott was hardly a settled community, and the land there was very dry. Nothing could be cultivated—we had to order fruits and vegetables from California. The white-washed houses were made out of mud. The barracks were miles from Prescott, and we had to trudge to school on a rough road. Fiorello would always play the "leader," and Richard and I always had to follow him. On the way we would sometimes meet Indians, Chinese workers, and most glamorous of all— the cowboys.

My father formed a musical club for his pupils. There were twelve of us boys and girls in the club. Fiorello played the cornet, Richard, the piano, and I played the violin. The club was most successful, and we played for many benefit programs.

Our summer vacations provided us with the happiest recollections. Every child of the regiment was given the use of the donkeys and tents. We would pack up and go up [to] the mountains. Fiorello always wanted to be the cook, and he was

very good at it. I can still taste the delicious fried potatoes that
were his specialty.

We attended high school at Prescott, and it was here that we
were taught by our beloved Miss Lena Coover. On September
20, 1947, when Fiorello was being mourned by all of New
York, Miss Coover flew from California to pay her respects to
her former pupil.

From Whipple Barracks we moved to Jefferson Barracks,
near St. Louis, Missouri. As we were boarding the regiment's
special train we heard a great commotion. An intoxicated soldier refused to get on the train because the train's serial number had a couple of thirteens in it. He screamed we would all be
unlucky. He was forced bodily off the train, and off we went.

It took five days and nights to reach St. Louis from Prescott
in those days. Halfway there the drunken soldier's prophecy
came true, for the commanding officer received a telegram an-
nouncing that war had broken out between America and
Spain.

It was 1898. The United States battleship *Maine* had blown
up in the harbor of Havana, Cuba, then a Spanish colony.[3] In
the weeks since, war jitters had been spreading across the coun-

---

3. On February 15, 1898, a mysterious explosion that destroyed the USS
Maine helped lead the United States into war against Spain. The *Maine*'s
mission was to protect American lives and property if Cuba's struggle for in-
dependence from Spain escalated into war. Of the 350 people aboard the
Maine, 266 were killed, and the press in the United States claimed the cause
was a mine or torpedo. After an official U.S. investigation agreed, Congress
formally declared war on Spain on April 25, 1898. By the end of that summer, Spain handed over Cuba (as well as the Philippines, Puerto Rico and
Guam) to the United States. A 1976 investigation determined that the explosion was internal, probably the result of a coal-bunker fire.

try, and my father had been worrying about what this might bring. Suddenly his regiment was ordered to proceed to Mobile, Alabama. The families of its men were to remain in Jefferson Barracks.

Our first glimpse of St. Louis, with the splendid Mississippi flowing past it, was spoiled. Everyone was shocked by the news and sad at the separation. A house was assigned to each family, and within an hour the men had to take their farewells from their loved ones.

I was fifteen years old at the time, and, being the only daughter, my father's pet.[4] He used to call me his "Sunshine." After Papa took leave from each of us, he rushed out of the door without looking back.

We had been in the town only one hour, and none of us knew how to get about. But I was determined to see Papa once more, so I dashed out, too. As it's the custom of the army to distract the people from their grief of parting with gay band music, I could hear the drums and tubas, and I followed the sound to the station. Among the thousands of soldiers I spotted Papa immediately and rushed into his arms.

We were given a nice two-storied little house, and my mother furnished it simply. Jefferson Barracks was a staging area where regiments were formed and shipped off to the war. One evening shortly after a large group had left, leaving only a few soldiers behind, a fire broke out in our neighbor's home. As the wooden houses were built close together, in a row, there was real danger that they would all soon be in flames. But Fiorello, who was fourteen then, grabbed his cornet and

---

4. Gemma was born on April 24, 1881, so she would have been sixteen in February 1898.

played the fire alarm, which brought aid and saved the houses.[5] This made him very popular at Jefferson Barracks.

One day Fiorello asked Mother for permission to go to Mobile to be near Papa. My mother hated to have him leave home, so she told Fiorello that she couldn't afford to send him there. He didn't say any more about the subject, but a few days later he visited the office of a St. Louis [news]paper. I think it was the *Dispatch*. He offered his services as a camp reporter with the 11th Infantry, telling the editor that Father was the regiment's bandmaster and that he, Fiorello, had a camera and so he could take photos to send with his daily report. The newspaper gave him the job, had a uniform made for him, and sent him to Mobile.

Every day Mother and I waited eagerly for the newspaper with Fiorello's articles. Papa was glad to have him there with him and was very proud of him. The regiment was ordered to Tampa, Florida, where it was stationed for a long time, and then it was ordered to Puerto Rico. But just then my father was taken very ill from eating contaminated canned meat and was sent back home to St. Louis.

As we didn't know how seriously ill he was, we rejoiced at this reunion. His period of military service expired at this time, and Papa decided that we should go to Europe and settle in Trieste. Throughout Papa's military service in the United States he was given a six months' furlough every three years. On almost every furlough we would pack up and travel to Europe. In this way we saw many of the most important Euro-

5. Fiorello La Guardia was born on December 11, 1882. He was fifteen by the time the *Maine* blew up.

pean cities—in France, Belgium, Switzerland, and Germany. It was Papa's way of giving us children a liberal education.

My brothers and I were not at all enthusiastic at the prospect of being away from America for a long time.

We arrived in Trieste to find the city in mourning for the recently assassinated Queen Elizabeth of Austria.[6] We stayed with [maternal] Grandmother Fiorina [Luzzatto Coen] in her old-fashioned but quite comfortable home. After a short time in Trieste, we settled in nearby Capo d'Istria. There my father opened a tourist hotel, which drew its guests from many parts of Europe and from the United States. In the cosmopolitan atmosphere of this beautiful resort town I took up the study of the Italian and German languages.

Fiorello kept plugging away at the college books he had brought with him from America, preparing himself to enter the university some day. He was always so ambitious and smart that the American consul in Budapest hired him as his secretary, and later he was appointed the acting consul in Fiume.[7]

One year later, on his twenty-first birthday [on December 11, 1903], Fiorello became the consul's agent for immigration. This was the first big step in his career and the only one that my father lived to see. At this time Fiume became a very important port because of the great wave of emigration that

---

6. Until 1918, the city was part of the Austro-Hungarian Empire; it was given over to Italy at the end of World War I. Elizabeth, Empress of Austria and Queen of Hungary, was assassinated by an Italian anarchist on September 10, 1898, while she was visiting Switzerland.

7. At that time Fiume was part of Hungary. It was part of Italy between 1924 and 1945, and now is Rijeka, Croatia.

was just beginning. People began coming from all parts of the continent to Fiume to sail on the Cunard ships to the United States.

In his work Fiorello was diligent, honest, and fearless. Once a director of the Fiume branch of the Cunard Line asked my brother for permission for the stevedores to work on Sundays. Brother answered that the ship was flying the American flag and that the United States law does not permit work to be done on Sunday. The director then offered him a large bribe. My brother asked him to leave his apartment at once and offered to throw him out if he didn't move quickly.

While Fiorello was in Fiume, my dear father died at the age of fifty-four, in October 1904. My brother then took us to live with him in Fiume. We had a beautiful home, and Brother did everything he could to make us comfortable and happy. He took me everywhere to social affairs with him. Every Sunday he dragged me to the football match. He introduced the game to Fiume and was made the captain of the team.

After two years of this quiet life Fiorello came to my mother and said: "Don't be angry, Mother, but I'm going to return to New York." Poor Mama was surprised and sad. She said: "But you have such a good position here, why must you go away?" Brother replied: "I want to have a career and I haven't finished my university studies. The position I have here I'll be able to keep until I'm an old, old man but I won't get any higher. Oh, no, Mother, I am ambitious. I want to study and get somewhere in my own country. I want to be somebody and do something really worthwhile." And off he went to the United States.

He went to New York and got a job as a sales clerk for $10.00 a week. He studied hard and passed a civil [service] examination as an interpreter at Ellis Island, the immigration station in New York harbor where the authorities screened the people streaming into the United States from all over the world. Fiorello worked there for four years, mastering several languages and attending the university at night. He got his law degree and passed the bar examination. The rest of Fiorello La Guardia's career is well known throughout the world.[8]

Shortly after Fiorello left for America, my younger brother Richard got a job on the Cunard Line as an interpreter, for he also knew many languages. He made fifty trips back and forth and then married and settled in Trenton, New Jersey. Richard died of a heart attack at the age of forty-two, leaving a wife and three children.[9]

8. Among the many books specifically about or including Fiorello's history, Brodsky, *The Great Mayor* (2003), has an extensive bibliography and a chronology of his life.

9. Richard died on February 6, 1935, at age 47 *(Trenton Evening Times,* 1935).

2

A Happy Marriage

MOTHER AND I were left alone in Fiume. I withdrew from social life and was contented to live quietly with my mother. To help in supporting us I decided to work, and started English classes. I must say that I became an instant success, receiving so many applications that I often sent pupils to other teachers. I kept the same home and was able to give Mother all the comforts she needed. Our only amusement was to take a subscription to the opera, as we both loved music.

I taught in my own apartment. Most of my pupils were adults whom I taught singly or in groups of four. Soon I was teaching ten hours daily. Every fortnight I held "English Teas" in the evenings, which were very interesting social times. I gave lectures, taught reading and spelling, held contests and spelling bees, and gave dictation. There were always thirty or more people present. This was for me a pleasure—to increase the knowledge of English in such a far-away place as Fiume.

As young girls do, I also had several admirers and many offers of marriage. But when Papa was living it seemed no one was suitable enough for me. Then it was my brother Fiorello, who, when he noticed somebody paying too much attention to me, would chase the boys away. I will always say it's much easier for a man to make his destiny than for a girl. It seems to be always somebody else who makes it for her.

In Europe it was the custom for girls to bring a dowry to a marriage. As I had none, I always used to joke and tell my suitors that I could bring no money in marriage, but that I would bring three objects: a piano, a sewing machine, and my mother. I can tell you this statement was very effective, for in some cases I didn't see that suitor any more.

Among my scholars I had a very intelligent, kind Hungarian gentleman, Herman Gluck, and if somebody had told me then that he was going to be my husband, I would have laughed. But after we had known each other for a year and a half, he proposed, and I repeated to him, too, what my dowry would be. But he got the better of me, for he gave such good answers. When I said:

"I will bring the piano," he answered:

"Fine, when I'll come home tired, you'll play for me."

Then came the sewing machine. He answered:

"Why, of course! This we shall need, especially if we'll have children."

And then I said:

"You will have a mother-in-law in your home." He quickly answered:

"Do you think for a minute that I would ask you to marry me without your mother coming to live with us? We both need her."

I accepted him.

My advice to young girls is not to choose a husband for good looks. My husband was not at all handsome, but it is the character, the intelligence, diligence, and goodness of a man with which one should fall in love. This was true in my case. I wish that every girl could marry as well and live as happily as I did during thirty-six years of married life. Herman and I had love and tolerance for the ways in which we were different from one another.

We were married in my family's house. Out of respect for my husband's religion, the ceremony was performed by a rabbi. Herman was not a religiously observant man and often during our years in Budapest I had to remind him to go to the synagogue on the High Holy Days, especially on the Day of Atonement, which the Jews call Yom Kippur. On that holiest of days the synagogues of Budapest were filled to overflowing with people from every walk of life. As for myself, I used to go to church.[1]

Religion, both Christianity and Judaism, had been an important part of the early years of my life. I felt no inner conflict about the different forms of religious practice I used to see in my parents' house. In this respect, my father showed great understanding and he instilled it in his children. He insisted that we say the Hebrew prayer, "Sh[e]ma Yisrael" (Hear, O Israel), every evening at bedtime. We learned the prayer by heart and I remember it even now.

---

1. Although she was not a practicing Jew, Gemma was Jewish. Nazi "racial theory" considered as Jewish any person who had at least one Jewish grandparent. Jewish religious law considers as Jewish any person born of a Jewish mother, as were Gemma and Fiorello. Their maternal grandmother was Fiorina Luzzatto Coen, and their maternal grandfather was Abramo Isacco Coen. Their mother, Irene Coen La Guardia, was Jewish, and their father, Achille La Guardia, was born Catholic but identified himself as having no religion on his marriage certificate.

Teaching it to us was an expression of my father's deep love for my mother. He took pride in my mother's rich Jewish heritage and frequently used to remind us that our grandmother Fiorina was a Luzzatto—a member of one of Italy's most prominent Jewish families. It had produced many renowned scholars and famous soldiers and statesmen, who had made considerable contributions to the greatness of Italy.

It was as an expression of admiration for Grandmother Fiorina that my parents had named their firstborn son Fiorello.

For a short time after our marriage Herman and I lived in Fiume where he got a job as a bank employee. Then he was transferred to Budapest and we moved there. My mother came with us and the three of us lived together happily until Mother died in 1915. She lies buried in Budapest's Jewish cemetery, where her grave is marked by a modest stone bearing a two-line inscription: "Irene La Guardia, 1859–1915."

For many years my husband was employed by the largest rubber manufacturing company in Budapest. Then a manager from the rubber company joined the credit bank and he took my husband with him. Herman had an excellent position, and after work he made many translations of books, movies, and commercial correspondence in six languages.

Two children were born to us. In 1911 my daughter Yolanda, who was to share the experiences described in this book, was born. Seven years later my daughter Irene was born. After her birth, I began to teach English again and held the English conversation evenings with good results again in Budapest, too.

We had a lovely eight-room apartment. There were no luxuries, but it was very comfortable and attractive, with needlework and fresh flowers in every room. Our library had very interesting historical works, a beautiful collection of English literature, novels in six languages, and my husband's various translations, dictionaries, and technical books. We had several instruments, as Yolanda and Irene inherited our love for music. We had silverware, jewelry, money—and now all these things are only memories. The possessions acquired over a lifetime are all gone.

Our home was on Nagymezo Street, 43 11/5. This street was in a good location. The western railroad station was in back. Streetcars passed near our home. The telephone center was opposite to us. The beautiful Andrassy Street and the opera house were close by. Our street was a miniature of Broadway, for many theaters, night clubs, and cinemas were there.

I lived very happily in Budapest. I liked the people. They were so kind and hospitable, well educated, and ambitious. Many of the women were beautiful and dressed very tastefully. They had especially beautiful foot gear and lovely legs. The men made wonderful husbands, and the women were excellent housewives and marvelous cooks.

Budapest had fascinating places to visit, and the country life of Hungary was very interesting. I found that the Hungarians had great writers, sculptors, painters, actors, singers, and doctors. Their food and wines were superb. And the magic "gypsy music!" The musicians played with such feeling on their violins that they had the power to make a person cry or laugh.

I am glad that I lived in that beautiful former Budapest, and I'm glad that I'm not there now to see the difference.

I must say that next to my native city of New York I loved Budapest most. It had the same cosmopolitan atmosphere as New York, but without the hustle and bustle that can be so fatiguing. Today I live on the fringes of New York, in Long Island City, in a housing project built during my late brother's term as mayor of New York.

Now, in the sunset of my life, I find joy in the family that surrounds me. They are my daughters, Yolanda and Irene, and my grandchildren Richard, James, Gladys, and Clifford. Yolanda and Richard, her son, experienced the brutality of the Nazis as I did, but Irene, who had come to the United States before the war and married an American, was spared.[2]

The years since I came back to America have been good to me, but they cannot make up for the irreparable loss of my dear husband, who voluntarily accompanied me to the Calvary of the slave camps and perished there while I survived.

---

2. Irene Gluck came to the United States in 1938 and eventually married John Andrew Roberts. She came via Switzerland, where she had been part of a young women's string orchestra, playing the violin. She was a violinist with the City of New York Symphony Orchestra (conversation with Irene's daughter, Gladys Roberts McMilleon, June 24, 2004, New York).

3

Storm over Budapest

WAR CAME SLOWLY to Budapest. It didn't occur to me to worry about my family or friends even in the winter of 1943. Life went on smoothly in the capital of Hungary, although other European countries were crashing.

The anti-Semitic decrees promulgated by the Hungarian government were nominally based on the Nuremberg Laws, but they were not enforced as harshly as in Germany or in the other Nazi satellites.[1] It was significant that the Roman Catholic primate of Hungary, [Justinian] Cardinal Seredi, dared to speak out openly against the Nazi-like racial laws.

There was widespread belief among the people of Budapest that the Regent of Hungary, Admiral Nicholas Horthy, was at heart sympathetic to Great Britain, and his collaboration with the Germans was only a maneuver to keep his country from direct involvement in the war.

Of course the serenity was false, but there was no evident violence. The Germans requisitioned all our best provisions, and at that time Hungary had an abundance of everything—for example, grain, cattle, and wines. The Hungarian government

---

1. The Nuremberg Laws, enacted in Germany in September 1935, defined requirements for citizenship in the Third Reich, assured the purity of German blood and honor, and clarified the inferior position of Jews.

gave everything the Nazis asked for, with the hope that Hungary would be left out of the terrible war.

But as the war went on and food supplies grew short, the Nazis began to demand that Hungarian soldiers join the Nazi troops in their attacks upon the Soviet Union. Unwillingly, this was also granted as the government continued appeasement to keep Hungary itself from becoming a battleground.

The real trouble for Hungary began on March 19, 1944, the day the Nazis began full occupation of the country. Within a few hours the Germans took everything into their own hands. Premier Nicholas von Kallay was deposed and replaced by Ferenc Szalasi, leader of the Arrow Cross, the Hungarian Nazi party.[2] The government he formed immediately took all civil liberties away from the people. The Gestapo began at once to pilfer and to take possession of the villas, homes, and offices—throwing out the stunned Hungarians.

To describe what the Nazis did to the Hungarian Jews is heartbreaking. They took all the shops away from them; Jewish employees were forbidden to work in any offices. All the actors, artists, and musicians had to quit their engagements at once. Jewish doctors were allowed to practice only among the Jews; Christian doctors were not permitted to treat Jewish patients.

At the time my husband was employed by the Allgemeine Credit Bank, where he served as an accountant and handled correspondence in eight languages. Herman was highly respected in the firm, but after the Germans took over the bank

2. Pro-Nazi General Dome Sztojay succeeded Miklos Kallay as prime minister in March 1944, appointed by Hungarian Regent Horthy. Horthy then dismissed Sztojay in August. The Nazis forced Horthy to abdicate in October and installed a new Hungarian government under Ferenc Szalasi.

he lost his position because he was a Jew. Four men were needed to do his work at the bank, and the directors were very sorry they had to let Herman go. However, they continued to give him assignments to do at home, so the loss of his job was not too serious a hardship for us. And we were not anticipating any more trouble.

Then the Nazis started to step up the terror against Jews. A curfew was imposed and Jews were allowed on the streets only from 11 A.M. to 3 P.M.

Officially, the orders for persecution of Jews were issued by Hungary's pro-Nazi puppet government. It was common knowledge, however, that the instructions and directives were coming from the headquarters the Gestapo had established in the Majestic Hotel in the heart of Budapest.

Until this time liberal Hungarians and the country's Jews had been able to delude themselves that Hungary would escape the tragedies that had befallen the other parts of Nazi-occupied Europe. Muffled, as though coming through a thick wall of stone, echoes of the misfortunes of the enslaved populations of neighboring countries penetrated to us. Horrifying rumors of the ghettos, slave-labor camps, gas chambers, and crematoria, where millions had already perished, came through underground channels, but were received with skepticism.

Now the truth of it all came home to us, and we realized that we had lulled ourselves into a sense of security that was false. Even though their power was crumbling and their regime was in its final stages, the Nazis were about to apply to us—Jews and Christians alike—the methods of degradation, destruction, and mass murder they had been practicing, improving upon with typical German efficiency, in the other occupied countries.

After my husband and I had been taken away from Budapest, a ghetto was established there and the deportation of Jews to the extermination camps in Austria and Poland was begun.[3] Packed into freight cars like animals, without food or water and sometimes even without air, Hungary's Jews were shipped off to the slaughter.

Some cars had no destination; when they were pulled out of the city limits, the gas jets were turned on.[4] The friends and families of these poor victims never heard any more about them.

On May 12, 1944, I was ailing and in bed when Hungarian detectives at the order of the S.S. officers came into my home and held an investigation. They claimed that they had to search "for a particular object."

"Please tell me, what is the suspicious object?" I asked. One of them in a very important voice answered: "You will soon see what we are looking for."

In the middle of my bedroom they threw all of my linen, all of our clothing and personal belongings from all the wardrobes and chests of drawers. These things were heaped into a huge pile in the middle of the floor.

I was upset by this intrusion but not frightened, as I well

3. Camps in Austria were not defined as "extermination" camps, although many prisoners perished in concentration camps such as Mauthausen.

4. This sentence may refer to vans equipped to murder with carbon monoxide exhaust fumes, but the Hungarian Jews generally were deported to camps in Poland to be exterminated. Thousands of Jewish women were also sent to Ravensbrück in the fall of 1944. For background information on Hungary, see, for example, Yehil (1990, 501–20); Hilberg (1985, 796–860); and Braham (2000), as well as other volumes by Braham on Hungary.

knew that we had nothing hidden in our house that could be of any value to the Nazis. No one in my family in Budapest had been in any way connected in political activity or had attended any secret meetings.

The search lasted three hours, throughout all of the eight rooms, from attic to cellar. It was finally revealed that the investigators were hunting for a transmitter that they thought I was using to communicate with the mayor of New York City, my brother, Fiorello H. La Guardia.

Disgusted because they had no success, the men became angry and ill-tempered, for they couldn't earn merit with the Germans. They went into my pantry and took away all the provisions that I had been saving with great difficulty for the lean days we expected would come.

During this period bills had been posted throughout the city advising all citizens to store up food and other necessary articles. This was a sly trick of the Germans, who thereafter went into each home and demanded the stored-up provisions.

They robbed me of all the articles I had in my pantry, such as sugar, flour, fat, dried fruits. They filled their sacks with these things and then called out to my husband: "You dirty Jew, carry these sacks downstairs."

My husband replied with dignity: "If I were as young as you both are, I might take them down, but being sixty-three years old, I refuse." And he didn't take the overflowing bags downstairs.

We thought that with this pilfering we would be left in peace, but to our great surprise, after five of six days we received an official statement of penalty: We had to pay five hundred pengos for having had those articles in our pantry. After this incident we had one month of peace.

On June 7, 1944, at 9:30 P.M., I was arrested by four armed S.S. officers.[5] When they came to my home I asked them why I was being arrested. They answered: "You will soon return. We want only an interview with you." My frightened husband asked them for permission to escort me to the police station. They looked at each other and consented.

With shaking hands I dressed while an S.S. officer stood by. He did not permit me to speak alone to my daughter or to our servant. He instructed me to take some things with me and kept urging me to hurry. I lingered as long as I dared. I didn't want to leave my daughter, my son-in-law, and my three-month-old grandson, Richard.

When my husband and I were taken out from our home, we were driven to Buda and placed in different cells in the prison there.

Then I recalled that three days before my arrest an attractive lady had come to my home, for the purpose of stating that she was arranging to take English lessons from me. I asked her on what days and at what hours she wanted classes, if she had a particular grammar book, and other questions of interest to a pupil. But she made no answers to these questions and instead spoke in such a puzzling fashion that I became a little suspicious. She said that she hadn't decided whether to study English or German. Of course, afterward I understood that she wanted to trick me into speaking against the German language, but I had replied merely, "The student must decide

5. Gemma wrote here that she was arrested by S.S. officers, but in a questionnaire *(Fragebogen)* that she answered in Berlin in January 1946, she wrote she had been arrested in Budapest by the Gestapo (RA-Nr. I/3–3–10, MGR).

before coming to the teacher," and that both languages were useful.

Then with a beguiling smile the young woman said: "You know, I have just heard that your brother is the mayor of New York. Is that true?" I answered shortly: "Yes." She continued: "Isn't it funny, so many girls are crazy for film stars, but I don't care for them. I'm only crazy about your brother."

I smiled and said: "You are really a foolish young girl, as my brother is quite an old man." Then I became a little angry and said: "Please, I have no time for personal conversations." She stood up and said: "Well, everything is all in order. I shall begin my lessons tomorrow." I never saw her again.

However, on the following day the foremost Nazi newspaper in Budapest came out with a long, haranguing article which had as its theme: "How can the Hungarians permit the sister of Mayor Fiorello La Guardia, Hitler's greatest enemy, to live in Budapest?" The innocent-looking young flapper must have been either a Nazi reporter or a spy.

We, perhaps, would never have seen that article, for Nazi newspapers never came into our home, had it not been for a peculiar coincidence. On that day my husband was walking along one of the finest streets of Budapest, the Andrassy, and the wind was blowing sharply. A newspaper was rolling along the sidewalk, buffeted by the wind, and continually going toward Herman's feet. Finally he picked it up to throw it aside when my name in headlines caught his eye. It was this front-page "scoop" that was the immediate cause of our arrest.

After five days at the prison in Buda, and after having filled out numerous questionnaires and having answered a thousand questions, my husband and I were taken away by a route unknown to us. This was a specialty of the S.S.—never to tell the prisoner where he was going. The S.S. officers informed us that in due respect to my brother we would not be compelled to travel as other prisoners did—in freight cars—but that, instead, we would ride in a second-class compartment, escorted by two members of the S.S.

After we had traveled for some time I asked my husband if he had any idea where we were going. He told me that he had noted that we were on the Vienna train. And so we were. We arrived in Vienna late in the night and then had to wait for another train. I had become terribly thirsty, as is my wont when nervous, and I politely asked the stationmaster for a glass of water. He refused me harshly and forbade us to sit on the waiting-room benches. He ordered my husband and me to stand with our faces to the wall until our train came in.

We continued our journey and arrived at a very late hour at Linz. By that time my thirst was unbearable and I again attempted to get a glass of water. This time the stationmaster was a young man, and thank God, a kind person. He looked at the yellow star my husband was obliged to wear, and pointing at it he said: "We people of Linz bear no hatred for this." And he brought me a clean glass of water, saying: "Here you are, Mutti." We were forced to wait there until the police station opened in the morning. We were both very weak and tired by the time we arrived at Mauthausen at 2 P.M. the following day.

Mauthausen, which was a two-hour ride from Linz, was a beautifully situated establishment. But the camp was a terrifying place, just like a fortress. Everywhere were S.S. guards. Continually there was the sound of their high voices, screaming, and ill-treating the prisoners.

When we entered the office there several officers gathered around us and one of them took out a magazine, flipped some pages, and suddenly pointed to a picture in it. Looking sharply at me, he asked: "Do you know who this man is?" I answered proudly, "Yes."

"Do you know that he is one of Germany's greatest enemies?"

"Is he?" I asked.

"When did you see your brother last?"

"Twenty years ago," I told them.

They smiled among themselves and said to me: "Well, you will soon see him." When I asked when and how, they looked straight into my eyes and said: "We are going to bring your brother to Berlin soon, and he shall hang, while you, his sister, shall stand by and watch him hang."

I presume they were making this threat to frighten me into revealing some kind of information. My husband and I were then thrown into separate cells, next to each other. The sound of the closing of that iron door still rings in my ears.

Before separating us the guards confiscated all our possessions. The Nazi in the main camp office took my husband's gold watch and chain from him and our wedding rings from both of us.

Angry, I asked the man: "Haven't you a wife or a sister or a mother who wears something like these? Don't you know what they mean to us? Please, if you have a heart, give us back the rings."

He looked at me with a sinister expression, then ordered me to leave.

In the ring Herman had given to me was engraved a sentence from Shakespeare *(The Merchant of Venice)*: "Love me and leave me not." In the ring I had given him was inscribed: "Love me forever."

Mauthausen was one of the worst men's camps. In 1944, when I was there, no other women were in this prison. Later, when prisoners crowded in from all countries, and the other camps were all filled up, women were sent here also.

I was ordered to wear the men's striped uniform and such heavy wooden shoes (naturally no stockings) that I could hardly walk in them. The walls of the cells were so thick that when I knocked on them with my heavy wooden shoes my husband could not hear me reassuring him that I was nearby.

After a week of coarse treatment I was informed that the authorities could not let me remain in a men's camp, therefore I would have to go farther on. When the S.S. men led me away from Mauthausen, I begged them to let my husband know that I was being sent to another camp, for I didn't want him to think that I was going to be killed. The S.S. men laughed.

I was taken to Linz again, and on June 29 I was sent to Berlin. As usual, I was accompanied by two guards. Upon arrival (after having traveled the whole night) I was registered at the Gestapo's prison in Prince Albert Strasse. Then the two detectives were curious to see the city and the destruction made by the bombs, so they took an auto ride. They took me along with them and while driving through the city and looking at the destruction which was really terrible, they tormented me by saying: "Look and see what your cultured Americans have done."

Of course I didn't answer but I wanted to say: "Who has

started this? And what about Germany's barbarism?" But I had to keep my mouth closed. After going about the principal streets for over an hour we proceeded on our journey to Ravensbrück.[6]

6. Gemma wrote that she arrived in Ravensbrück on June 29, 1944. The directive to hold her as a political hostage rather than sending her to a death camp was issued on June 6, 1944 (Eichmann Trial document, letter from von Thadden, TR3 516, YV). According to the questionnaire *(Fragebogen)* that Gemma answered in Berlin in January 1946, the date of her arrival was June 30, 1944 (RA-Nr. I/3–3–10, MGR).

4

Ravensbrück—Hell for Women

"Deep into that darkness peering, long I stood there, wondering, fearing."

—Edgar Allan Poe, *The Raven*

THE APPROACH TO RAVENSBRÜCK, which was the Nazis' biggest concentration camp for women, was pleasant and picturesque. The road ran by flower beds planted by its [the camp's] prisoners. There were dark patches of pine woods and a calm blue lake.

The landscape changed suddenly as the high concrete walls of the camp and its barbed-wire fence loomed on the horizon. The first living creatures one encountered at the entrance to Ravensbrück were the large black ravens who swooped down with a shrill cackling that filled my heart with terror. Sometimes their chatter mingled with the sharp barking of police dogs.

The Nazis erected Ravensbrück on reclaimed swampland near the city of Fürstenberg, about fifty miles from Berlin, in the vicinity of the great Siemens industrial complex, thus providing slave labor for its electrical, chemical, and steel plants.[1]

---

1. Siemens, then known as Siemens und Halske, was the company that most exploited the slave labor of Ravensbrück's female prisoners. Siemens built a factory in a separate camp adjoining the main Ravensbrück camp in

Ravensbrück was intended to hold only 15,000 inmates, but by the time I arrived there it contained 40,000 women from all parts of Nazi-occupied Europe. It has been estimated that more than 120,000 women went through this hell. Only a small fraction survived.[2]

In the final phase of the war, as the Russian armies approached the slave-labor camps in Poland, the Germans began bringing huge transports of women to Ravensbrück from Majdanek, Auschwitz, and Sobibor. When there was no more room in its overcrowded barracks, they put up a huge tent. Straw was strewn on the earth for beds.[3]

It was like a circus but one without clowns—a circus where crying was heard and no laughter. The blocks were all jammed. Most of them had 1,200 to 1,500 women. Every seven women had to sleep in two adjoining beds (with only one blanket and one pillow on each bed). There were no chairs to sit on. Everywhere there were dirt, unhealthy odors, fleas, lice, and other vermin.

In the tent enclosure the women were nearly naked, hungry, and ill. We other prisoners took from ourselves a warm pair of knickers or a sweater, and as we were not permitted to go near them, we threw whatever we had at them. What an awful sight! They fought and pulled their hair and kicked one another away so that they could get at the article thrown to them.

1942 and "hired" the women to make electrical components for V-1 and V-2 rockets. See Saidel (2004, 95–100).

2. Records are incomplete, but the estimate most often used is 132,000 prisoners, with only 17,000 surviving.

3. For more information on the tent, including survivor testimony, see Saidel (2004, 18–19, 21, 80, 88, 132, 135).

An odor of putrefaction permeated that area. There was a typhoid epidemic and the dead were allowed to lie about during the day; the eighty or a hundred corpses that accumulated every day were taken to the crematory only at night.[4]

As criminals were also imprisoned in the concentration camps, one found many thieves among the prisoners. For this reason the small, insignificant, but precious possessions which we had—our spoons, our combs, our daily portions of bread—always had to be carried about wherever we went. Much pilfering was done when the prisoners slept. Although the criminals were given more power and were liked better than the political prisoners by the camp officials, still certain positions or occupations were given to political prisoners because they were more reliable.

When a woman arrived in Ravensbrück, she was taken to the baths—fifty to sixty women at a time took a shower. This was not done for the sake of cleanliness but to rob the prisoner of all that she brought with her—for example, clothes, jewels, underwear, money, and papers. And in exchange we received such [inappropriate] shoes and dresses that we all resembled so many beggars. They managed to give to a thin woman a fat woman's dress so that it would hang on her, or vice versa. Our uniforms in Ravensbrück were blue with gray stripes and our shoes had wooden soles. Later we were allowed to wear our own clothes with a large X painted on the back.[5] For the women who worked in the kitchen and in the office there were

4. Many survivors mistakenly use the term *typhoid,* but typhus was the disease prevalent in the camp.

5. As Gemma pointed out, the women's clothes were taken from them upon entry. As a special status prisoner, she had the privilege of having her

blue aprons. On the sleeves of our dresses and coats we had to wear a sign to distinguish why we were arrested, and underneath this our number, as we were not known by our names, only by numbers. This was Ravensbrück's method, and we considered ourselves lucky, for in some other camps they tattooed the number on the arm.

All prisoners wore on their sleeves small, triangular patches of cloth. The different colors were a code indicating the reasons for imprisonment.

Red was for political offenders.

Black was for socially undesirable persons—prostitutes and people who refused to work. Gypsies, as non-Aryans, were counted in this category.[6]

Purple was for the *Bibelforscherinen* ("Bible Students"), as the Jehovah's Witnesses sect is known in Germany.

Green represented the common criminals.

Yellow represented the Jewish religion.

Yellow and black represented *Rassenschande*—meaning a disgrace to the race.

According to the Nuremberg Laws from September 1935, it was forbidden to marry a Jew in Germany. If someone married a Jew in another country after the German occupation, the marriage was not valid. Therefore, these people were considered to have committed *Rassenschande*—disgrace to the race.

After they took all my belongings away, I was taken to Block Twenty-four, the "Quarantine Block," which held over 1,000

---

own clothing returned to her. The X on the back was to identify anyone who tried to escape.

6. Those arrested as lesbians were also considered "asocial" and wore the black triangle.

women. There was such noise that no one could rest either by day or night. There were women of all nationalities, and every language was heard. It was the rule that each prisoner after her arrival had to remain in this block in quarantine for one month and was not permitted to go out except for the morning roll call. I am sure if I had to remain in this block a longer time I couldn't have lived.

Only six days later, on July 4, the commander of the camp ordered that I should be taken out of this block and immediately brought to Block Number Two. I was a greenhorn and I didn't know anything about the different blocks, therefore I was frightened at what they would do with me. Only afterward I was told that Blocks One and Two were the "elite" blocks. In Block Three were mostly Communists, and these three blocks were the cleanest and considered the best of the whole camp, as each had only about four hundred prisoners and not twelve hundred to fifteen hundred like the other blocks.

I was told that I was lucky and could thank my brother for it. I asked why, and they replied: "On account of your brother, you have been made a *Sonder-Häftling*, a special prisoner." I had already observed that although they hated Fiorello as an enemy, still, they either respected or feared him.

Being a special prisoner meant that I didn't have to work twelve hours daily like the other poor women, and also I had a bed for myself. Besides, I was permitted to rest one hour in the afternoon. But that was all, as the food I received was what all the others got. We ate *Steckrüben* (turnips) cooked with potato peelings for our dinner. For breakfast and supper we had black coffee with a piece of a terrible black bread which many times had great holes gnawed in it by the rats.

In the first months of my arrest, at the time the S.S. were

looting in all the different countries, we were given some imitation honey and sometimes a sort of marmalade. On Saturday evenings we were given a piece of a very smelly "cheese" made from potatoes. On Sunday, a piece of sausage. But in the last months we received only dried bread. We had to divide this daily portion so that we had enough for the whole day. One loaf had to be divided into four parts for four persons. When scarcity came, we had to divide it into five or six parts. For me this terrible food was sufficient, but the poor women who had to work hard for twelve hours a day suffered terribly from hunger.

I was appointed supervisor of the packages. Our block daily received fifty or sixty packages. They were chiefly Red Cross packages sent mostly to the French, Polish, and Czech prisoners. Many of these packages came from Switzerland, Canada, Denmark, and Czechoslovakia, sent by parents, relatives, or good friends. As none of my family knew where I was, of course I never received a package.[7] At the end these packages came nearly empty, as their contents were stolen in the post office.

In the evening the officials were seen with the women overseers, drinking together the tea or coffee and eating the sweets that had been sent to the prisoners. But if a prisoner stole a potato and had the ill luck to be caught, she was taken to the chief superintendent who would order her thrashed with a leather whip.

Ravensbrück became a sort of industrial center. Here articles could be manufactured cheaply. As it didn't cost the Gestapo anything—the prisoners had many high skills and

---

7. Jewish prisoners generally did not receive packages because they had no family left behind at home.

worked well with little food—if the work was not well done, severe punishments were given. There were two shifts. The poor prisoners had to work twelve hours every day for a week, and during the next week these women slept by day and worked twelve hours at night.

The dressmaking department could have held a fashion show in any large city and the ladies of high fashion would have marveled at the styles and wonderful taste. Among the prisoners were professional dressmakers, designers, decorators. These prisoners were mostly French. Dresses and coats of all sorts were made, but the specialty were the evening gowns, which were sent to all the great German cities, chiefly to Berlin, to the wives or mistresses of the Gestapo officers. Then there were the tailor shops where the uniforms were made for the military services. The shoemaking department produced on a large scale, too. There was also a fur department. Here it was stupefying to see what beautiful collections of fur coats were created. They even manufactured fur toy animals, such as bears and monkeys.

The women of the camp also practiced other trades. We had carpenters, painters, plumbers, blacksmiths, electricians. The laundry was furnished with the most modern equipment. The camp officials selected the fine, intelligent nuns to work in the laundry.

Polish women were mostly assigned to work in the kitchens. Then there was the police force. Here the strongest, roughest, and most heartless women were selected. The most intelligent women (nearly all political prisoners) were selected for the office work, library, and post office. Women over sixty years of age had to knit.

I, being a "special prisoner," didn't have to work, but after the first week passed I felt terrible not to be doing something among these overworked women. I requested to be appointed a *Tischälteste* (supervisor of a dining table). The tables were so arranged that, for example, all Poles sat at one table, Italians at another, and the Germans had a table for themselves.

I asked to have the privilege to select the prisoners for my table. They asked me why. I replied: "For no other reason than I should like to have an international table." They granted me this, but warned me that I would have a very difficult time with people of different nationalities. I answered: "I think it'll be interesting and I wish to try."

I'm very proud to say that my idea worked out so well that the camp officials came often to observe my table.

I had thirty-four women of twelve different nationalities and of several religions at my table. It was long and very narrow and served about fourteen persons comfortably. We had two shifts for eating. At noon the workers of the laundry ate and at twelve-thirty came the political prisoners from the offices. Sometimes the debates waxed hot, and it was exciting to hear the different opinions when they discussed politics. Then I had to become a peacemaker. I had Russians, Czechs, Poles, Norwegians, Yugoslavs, Italians, French, and Hungarians. Many of them could speak two of these languages. Twelve of my women were Bible Students.

My duties were simple but important. I had to divide the bread into thirty-four equal portions, the soup into thirty-four bowls. The dishes and cupboards for them had to be scrubbed clean.

Once a month we were permitted to write to our families. Writing letters to our dear ones outside was a great moment in the bitter monotony of camp life. Each of us used to stretch her imagination to convey some indication of her true feelings and her worries safely past the censor. I took upon myself the task of procuring post cards, writing paper, and stamps for the women at my international table.

Our letters were collected by an overseer. We had no way of knowing whether they reached their destinations because we seldom received mail in Ravensbrück. The few replies to our letters that did come had little "windows" cut out by the censors. Even the slightest of hints about how things were going at home was eliminated.

Each month I had to make an inventory of the prisoners' clothes. Having the greatest number of prisoners at my table, I was very much occupied, but I did my work with love for "my children." They reciprocated my affection and called me "Mutti," which means "Mother" in German. How often they confided their sorrows to me and asked for advice.

5

Underground English Classes

IN THE AFTERNOON, during my free time, I gave lessons in English. These were the most gratifying hours I spent in Ravensbrück. Having no grammar book, I wrote one myself and made thirty copies for my pupils. I still have one of them. It is a hundred pages long. On the concluding pages I wrote several short prayers of my own composition and a number of proverbs.

We had to study in secrecy, of course. If we had been caught, all of us would have been severely punished, especially the teacher. We used to post a lookout to signal us if any of the overseers approached. Paper and pencils were stolen for us by inmates who worked in the camp office.

My students were girls and women from many different nationalities. Most of them were eager to learn English because they dreamed of going to the United States after liberation.

There were two classes, one for beginners and a conversation class for the more advanced, those who had once studied English in school or had picked up some knowledge of the language in other ways.

I took pride in the fact that these women, from so many different walks of life, returned the affection I came to have for them. They were grateful for the things I was able to do for them and showed it in many ways.

Among my pupils were also a few Russian women. There were a considerable number of them in Ravensbrück. They were kept in separate barracks. Most of them were Red Army personnel, captured on the Eastern Front, and there were many doctors and nurses among them.

We often heard them singing Russian songs, and admired their solidarity and discipline, but they were reserved and seldom spoke to other prisoners. They seemed to distrust us, despite the fact that all were sharing the same fate at the hands of the Nazis. This was probably the result of their upbringing and rigid training by their party.

As their contacts with us increased, their aloofness gradually disappeared. They were particularly attracted by the underground educational activities going on in the camp, and some joined my English classes. I was amazed by their facility with languages.

The overseers used Russian and Ukrainian girls for the dirtiest and most exhausting jobs in camp. They belonged to the *Kübel-Kolonne,* the garbage collectors. They were also forced to dig the ditches that served as a sewage system.

The Nazis did everything they could to keep their prisoners divided by creating animosity among the different nationalities, but they did not succeed. The barriers of language broke down as did those of social position and upbringing. We really became one family, united by our sufferings and our hopes.

At the camp we were not known by name, only by number. Each prisoner had her number sewn upon the sleeve of her dress and coat. Mine was 44,139. When called before the superintendent or overseer, one had to stand at attention and say: "Prisoner 44,139."

I am a soldier's daughter and would never have minded standing at attention before a superior, but to have to do so before these S.S. women, most of whom had been criminals or perhaps prostitutes in civilian life, was terrible punishment. The overseers were a bunch of rotters, cruel-hearted, ignorant, taking pleasure in torturing the poor prisoners.

The cruelest of all was the chief superintendent, S.S. Oberaufseherin Dorothea Binz. She had a well-deserved reputation for bestiality, for which she paid the penalty on the gallows in 1947. Dorothea Binz was one of eleven supervisors and doctors at Ravensbrück who were sentenced to death by hanging at the Hamburg War Crimes Trials in the British Occupation Zone of Germany.

There were, however, one or two of the overseers in Ravensbrück who had a heart. I personally spoke to one who complained that she was forced to join the S.S., the Nazi elite corps, which committed the worst crimes.

There were many mothers with children in Ravensbrück. The little ones, of whom at one time there were perhaps five hundred, added a note of special horror and tragedy to the atmosphere of the camp. They looked like little skeletons wearing rags. Some had no hair on their heads. Nevertheless, they behaved like children, running around and begging things from their elders. They even played games. A popular one was *Appell,* modeled on the camp's daily roll calls.

Most of the children lived in the barracks along with their mothers. I remember one Hungarian Jewish woman who had four, ranging in age from four to twelve. All five—mother and children—had to sleep in one bed. The children were beautiful, and their mother kept them very clean.

There were also pregnant women in Ravensbrück. Most of them were German nationals accused of *Rassenschande* [literally, "race shame" or "disgrace to the race," a term used to refer to a sexual union between an "Aryan" and a "non-Aryan."]. Babies were born in the *Revier* (infirmary). I used to hear the screams of the mothers in labor and the wails of the newborn, most of whom were to die very shortly. The callous camp nurses would put five or six infants into a single crib and inevitably they would smother one another.

Once I saw a Nazi guard carrying a bag slung over his shoulder.

"Know what I have here?" he asked cynically, pointing to the bag. "Dead babies."

But, miraculously, a few of the babies lived to leave Ravensbrück when their mothers were liberated.

6

Comrades in Misfortune

IN THE MULTITUDE of women the Nazis had herded together in Ravensbrück there was a great variety of nationalities and social types, and many individuals whom I found very interesting. Their reactions to the inhuman conditions under which they lived were a fascinating study in human nature.

I discovered that true comradeship can develop among those subjected to such conditions. In that dreadful place we were all equals. There was no wealth, no titles, no envy to divide us. I came to know a great many people, but there were five or six women to whom I was particularly close and whom I shall always remember.

One was Mrs. Lotti Lehman (Silverman) who on a bitter winter morning did me an unforgettable act of kindness.[1]

For some reason we never learned, the guards decided to hold morning roll call at four o'clock, instead of the usual hour of five. Chilled and benumbed, I stood in line with the others in the predawn blackness. The frost pierced me to the marrow.

Lotti noticed my shivering. "What's the matter with you, Mutti?" she asked.

---

1. The correct name is Silbermann. A short article by Lotte Silbermann appears in Schwarz and Szepansky (2000).

"I haven't any underwear. I'm freezing." My voice quavered with cold and fear.

After the *Appell*, when we came back into the barracks, Lotti took off her underwear and handed it to me. At first I refused to accept it. It was too great a sacrifice. But she insisted, and eventually I took the garment.

Lotti came of a well-to-do family in Berlin. In Ravensbrück she worked in the dressmaking shop, which turned out beautiful clothes for the wives and sweethearts of Nazi officers. The finest fabrics—velvets, silks, brocades—were brought here from occupied France, together with skilled seamstresses and designers who had been arrested on the slightest pretexts.

Another who showed me unusual devotion and readiness to help was Annamarie Thiel, now Robertson, a charming, young blond German girl who had been in Ravensbrück since September 1943. Annamarie had been sent to the concentration camp because she helped her Jewish neighbors in Berlin. She worked in the camp office, and one of her duties was to distribute the Nazi party newspaper, *Völkischer Beobachter*, among the camp officials and overseers.

We prisoners were not permitted to read anything from outside, not even the official Nazi organ. This ban was very harshly enforced during the last period of the war when one could find, even in the party newspaper, clear hints of the Nazi defeats on the war fronts. Annamarie used to risk her life to bring us not only the *Völkischer Beobachter*, but also provincial newspapers. These were more outspoken about the turn of events that spelled defeat for the Nazis.

Hilde Brook, a chemist from Danzig, had been arrested in 1942 because she was helping to hide people—Jews and non-

Jews—wanted by the Gestapo. After many months in jail at Potsdam and in the infamous Moabit prison in Berlin, she was shipped to Ravensbrück in March 1943. Hilde also worked in the camp office. She had charge of the so-called "lager" money.

On arrival at Ravensbrück every prisoner had to surrender all her possessions, including money. Once a month she was permitted to withdraw a certain sum paid out in scrip which was called *Lagergelt* [camp money]. One could buy whatever was available in the canteen, but there was very little choice. Sometimes there was herring, or a piece of candy, or salt, which was a great luxury. Usually, however, there were only trinkets and junk that was of no use.

I was never inside the canteen, because I had not brought any money to Ravensbrück and no *Lagergelt* was issued to me.

Both Annamarie and Hilde live in New York now, and they visit me every year on my birthday.

There was also Odette Garoby, the wife of a French sea captain from Algiers. On my first day in our block, when I was filled with misery and despair, I suddenly heard a beautiful voice singing "Swanee River." To hear this familiar song, with the English words rendered in a charming French accent, was very comforting to me. I stood enchanted, and then spontaneously joined the singer: "Way down upon the Swan-ee River, far, far away . . ."

At the end of the song we introduced ourselves. From that first encounter emerged a friendship that has been deep and lasting, despite differences in our ages and dispositions. She was very chic and witty and could come up with a joke in the most dismal situation.

Odette had been arrested on the street in Paris during a

routine roundup by the Nazis in the wake of a sabotage action by the underground. She was taken away and shipped to Ravensbrück without any opportunity to advise her husband and family of her whereabouts.

Among the inmates of Ravensbrück was a small, frail woman with a great heart whose conduct gave encouragement to us all. Everybody knew Dr. Gertrud Luckner and came to her seeking help and advice.

Even our Nazi overseers—the "ravens" of Ravensbrück, we called them, because of the black capes they wore—showed her respect, apparently in recognition of her status as an internationally known social worker. For years Dr. Luckner had been the heart and soul of a Catholic charitable institution, the Caritaszentrale, in Freiburg, and gave assistance to the victims of National Socialism. In the Ravensbrück concentration camp she used her privileges to bring aid and comfort to the neediest among us.

Gertrud Luckner was born in Liverpool, but she had lived in Germany from early childhood. She received her higher education in Germany and also attended the College for Religious and Social Work, operated by the Quakers at Woodbrooke in England. After receiving her doctorate Gertrud Luckner worked at the headquarters of the Deutscher Caritaszentrale (German Welfare Association) in Freiburg. Dr. Conrad Groeber, the archbishop of Freiburg, who was responsible for the charitable activities of the German episcopate, entrusted her with the delicate task of administering whatever aid could legally be given to those who suffered under National Socialism, especially the Jews.

At the same time, as the Nazi terror fastened its grip on Germany, Dr. Luckner began on her own initiative to give its victims whatever assistance she could, whether or not it was within the law. Tirelessly and unobtrusively, she traveled through Germany and the occupied territories that were incorporated into the Greater Reich. She was a frequent visitor to ghettos and concentration camps, bringing comfort and financial help to Jew and Christian alike.

Dr. Luckner maintained close contact with Dr. Leo Baeck, chief rabbi of Berlin, and with the Jewish communities all over Germany. On a visit to Cologne in August 1941, she learned from the rabbi of its Jewish community, Dr. Caro, that it was possible to mail money orders in amounts up to ten marks into the ghetto of Litzmannstadt, as the Nazis had renamed the Polish city of Lodz. She began collecting money and, bit by bit, transmitted the money to the Jews penned up in the Litzmannstadt ghetto.

Thoroughly imbued with the ideal of the brotherhood of mankind, Gertrud Luckner risked her life by continuing activities the Nazis declared illegal. She was arrested in March 1943, on a train while traveling on one of her missions of mercy. She was turned over to the Gestapo in Dusseldorf, and after nine weeks of questioning and several months in a Gestapo prison Dr. Luckner was sent to Ravensbrück. She was one of the first inmates with whom I became acquainted when I arrived there in the spring of 1944.

There was little Gertrud Luckner could do to alleviate the plight of the prisoners of Ravensbrück, but the mere presence of this noblest of women brought us courage in the darkest hours of our lives. To us she was a tower of strength in the midst of that sea of hatred and brutality.

It is gratifying to know that the years of persecution by the Nazis did not break her indomitable will. In the truest spirit of forgiveness, she returned to Caritas in Freiburg to continue her charitable work among the German people and her untiring efforts to strengthen friendship between Christians and Jews.[2]

There was in our block a pretty young girl who was a mystery to us. She kept to herself and hardly spoke a word. Yet every evening, after nine o'clock, when we were not allowed to talk and were supposed to be asleep, she would start to sing. Her voice was beautiful, and the tune was always the same: the Italian song "La Paloma." One night a German officer came into the barracks. We all became panicky, expecting the worst, but to our astonishment the Nazi said to her: "I don't mind your singing, but tell me why you sing the same song all the time?"

The girl broke her silence about her past long enough to tell the officer: "I promised my parents when I parted from them that this song would be my good-night kiss."

2. On February 15, 1966, Yad Vashem recognized Gertrud Luckner as Righteous Among the Nations.

7

Sad Christmas Celebration

ON CHRISTMAS EVE, 1944, we all assembled at our table
and tried in vain to put ourselves in a holiday mood. Some of
the women had brought along, as special delicacies, pieces of
candy they had managed to get at the canteen and tiny sandwiches made of bread and marmalade they had carefully saved.
But my heart was filled with sadness. Suddenly I could not
stand being at the table any longer.

"Please don't be angry," I said, "but I'm going to bed. I
cannot stop thinking of my family at this hour." I left the table.

The others followed me and sat around my bed. Then they
presented me with Christmas gifts they had obtained by all
kinds of personal sacrifices, even at the risk of their lives.

One of the women gave me a great luxury for Ravensbrück,
a pillow she had stolen somewhere in the camp. But the most
precious of the presents I received was a little album. It was put
together from sheets of paper smuggled out of the camp office
and bound in a piece of cotton print taken from the dressmaking shop.

They presented their gifts to me and said: "Mutti, we beg
you, come to the table with us. Let's celebrate Christmas." I
was overwhelmed by their display of affection but I mustered

all my strength and went with them to the table. We sang songs that lifted our spirits.

The little album they had given me passed from hand to hand and everyone wrote in it something in her own language. The first entry was by one of the Russians, the young and charming Katya, who signed herself "Katya Sibiriatchka" (Katya from Siberia). In Russian she wrote: "Dear Gemma: Nothing in life is impossible or too difficult to achieve if the will is strong. Even from Siberia to America is not too far. If you will not come to me, I will come to you."

At every opportunity in the months that followed the women would make entries into my album, often expressing their affection for me.

Dr. Gertrud Luckner made an entry in my album that started with a quotation from Goethe in German, followed by an ironic note in English: "Under the 'heaven' of R'bruck! Ships that pass in the night—and yet in loving memory. Gertrud Luckner, Freiburg Br. Caritasverband (via Society of Friends)."

The album was always carefully concealed in my stocking and I never parted with it. I was aware how terrible it would be for these poor women if that little book fell into the hands of the overseers.

Many wrote quotations from famous poets or verses composed by themselves in their native tongues. Some of my students tried to write in English, which they mastered rather quickly. The Poles were particularly good at this. One girl from Poznan, Christina Janicka, wrote this story in English: "Perhaps after many, many weeks you will take in your hands this album and you will remember 'R. Sanatorium.' Please, for a short moment look at my name and send me a few words. Let me know how you are, dear Mrs. Gemma Gluck. I want to thank you for the lovely moments we spent together studying English and thinking of our homes, our loved ones, and mostly of the future."

In a similar vein was the entry of the witty Odette Garoby. Writing in French, she expressed the hope that someday, after liberation, she would see me together with my husband, my daughters Irene and Yolanda, my grandson Richard, and my brother Fiorello.

A Polish girl from Cracow wrote these thoughts:

The measure of greatness in nations as in individuals is their patience. Our country and our people gave undeniable proof of this. Maybe someday I will be privileged to meet you again and then we will be able to look back into our sad past. In these last days of struggle I am writing these few words as a remembrance of our meeting and the lessons you gave us. Even in slavery and on foreign soil one can have pleasant memories. To these belong the moments I lived through with you in Block Two.

Danuta Tulmacka

An entry that brought back memories of my childhood in New York and filled me with hope for a return to my native city was written by Mrs. C. Bosch from the Netherlands: "I wish you all the best and happiness in the future. Hoping you will see the Statue of Liberty very soon."

Irene Coen La Guardia, Gemma's mother,
Watertown, New York, circa 1890. *Courtesy of the
LaGuardia and Wagner Archives.*

Achille La Guardia, Gemma's
father, in U.S. Army uniform,
Prescott, Arizona, circa 1895.
*Courtesy of the LaGuardia
and Wagner Archives.*

The La Guardia family and others with musical instruments,
Prescott, Arizona, 1896. *Courtesy of Sharlot Hall Museum,
Prescott, Arizona.*

Gemma La Guardia as a
young girl with violin,
Fort Whipple, Prescott,
Arizona. *Courtesy of the
LaGuardia and Wagner
Archives.*

Fiorello La Guardia at his graduation from law school, New York University, June 1910. *Courtesy of the LaGuardia and Wagner Archives.*

Richard La Guardia, Gemma and Fiorello's brother, circa 1929. *Courtesy of Richard La Guardia's granddaughter, Mary.*

Herman Gluck, Gemma's husband, with daughters Yolanda (left) and Irene in Budapest, 1930s. *Courtesy of Gladys McMilleon.*

Fiorello La Guardia, as mayor, laying cornerstone for Queens-bridge Houses in Long Island City, New York, April 26, 1939. Gemma lived there from 1947 until her death in 1962. *Courtesy of the LaGuardia and Wagner Archives.*

Mayor Fiorello La Guardia at a anti-Nazi rally in New York, circa 1944. *Courtesy of the LaGuardia and Wagner Archives.*

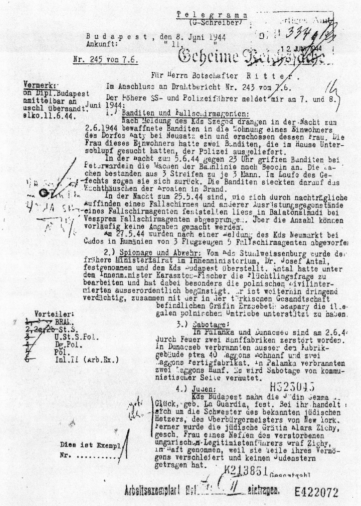

Nazi report of Gemma's arrest as a political hostage, 1944. *Courtesy of Gladys McMilleon.*

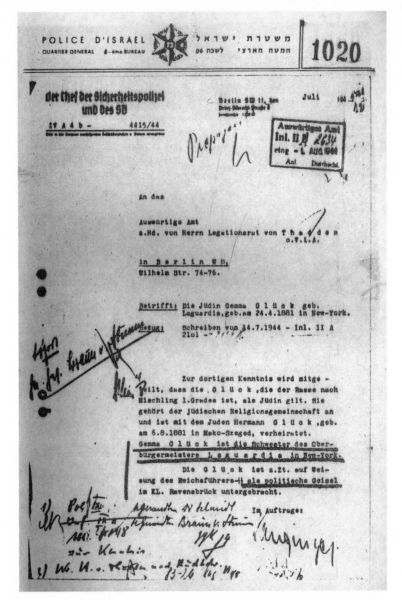

Der Chef der Sicherheitspolizei
und des SD

IV A 4 b -   4415/44

Berlin SW 11, den   Juli   194

An das

Auswärtige Amt
z.Hd. von Herrn Legationsrat von T h a d d e n
o.V.i.A.

in B e r l i n W 8,
Wilhelm Str. 74-76.

Betrifft: Die Jüdin Gemma G l ü c k geb.
Laguardia,geb.am 24.4.1881 in New-York.

Bezug: Schreiben vom 14.7.1944 - Inl. II A
2101 --

    Zur dortigen Kenntnis wird mitge -
teilt, dass die G l ü c k ,die der Rasse nach
Mischling 1.Grades ist, als Jüdin gilt. Sie
gehört der jüdischen Religionsgemeinschaft an
und ist mit dem Juden Hermann G l ü c k ,geb.
am 6.8.1881 in Mako-Szeged, verheiratet.
Gemma G l ü c k ist die Schwester des Ober-
bürgermeisters L a g u a r d i a in New-York.

    Die G l ü c k ist z.Zt. auf Wei-
sung des Reichsführers-H als politische Geisel
im KL. Ravensbrück untergebracht.

Im Auftrage:

Nazi police report about Gemma, July 14, 1944. Eichmann trial
document 1020. *Courtesy of Yad Vashem, Israel.*

Ravensbrück women's concentration camp, prisoner drawing of the Siemens factory, which Gemma described. *Courtesy of Mahn- und Gedenkstätte Ravensbrück.*

Crematorium and punishment block at Ravensbrück, both of which Gemma described. *Photo by Rochelle G. Saidel, 1995.*

Magistrat der Stadt Berlin / Abt. für Sozialwesen / Hauptausschuß „Opfer des Faschismus"

Mein Name: _Gemma Glück, geb. La Guardia_

Meine Anschrift: _Charlottenburg, Fritschestr. 69 I_

A. **Fragebogen**

I. Ich bin festgenommen worden:

Nr.	am?	Von welcher Stelle?	In welchem Ort?
1	7. 6. 1944	Gestapo	Budapest
2			
3			

II. Ich bin verurteilt worden:

Nr.	am?	Von welchem Gericht? Aktenzeichen? Namen des Staatsanwalts, des Richters?	zu welcher Strafe?	Wieviel davon verbüßt?
1				
2				
3				

III. Ich war in folgenden Gestapoquartieren, Untersuchungsgefängnissen, Straf-anstalten und Konzentrationslagern in Haft:

Nr.	vom	bis	in (möglichst genaue Bezeichnung der Gestapostelle oder Anstalt):
1	7.6.44	15.6.44	Gefängnis Budapest
2	16.6.44	22.6.44	Männer-Konzentrationslager Mauthausen
3	23.6.44	29.6.44	Linz - Gefängnis
4	30.6.44	15.IV.45	Frauenkonzentrationslager Ravensbrück
5	16.IV.45	21.IV.45	S.S. Gefängnis, Linz Albrechtstr. Berlin
6	22.IV.45	29.IV.45	Polizei-Präsidium Kaiserdamm, Charlottenburg
7			
8			

IV. Folgende Beamten haben die Gefangenen gequält und mißhandelt?

Nr.	Bezeichnung der Anstalt oder des KZ.	Name des Beamten (möglichst mit Anschrift)	Was hat er sich im einzelnen zuschulden kommen lassen?
1	wegen meines Bruders wurde ich als Sonderhäftling behandelt		
2			
3			
4			
5			
6			
7			
8			
9			
10			

HW 623

Fragebogen testimony by Gemma about her incarceration, 1946.
Courtesy of Mahn- und Gedenkstätte Ravensbrück.

Fiorello La Guardia with Kathryn Cravens, who brought news from Gemma in Berlin, 1945. *Photograph by the Acme News Agency, courtesy of Corbis.*

Gemma La Guardia Gluck with her daughters Irene and Yolanda, circa 1961. *Courtesy of Gladys McMilleon.*

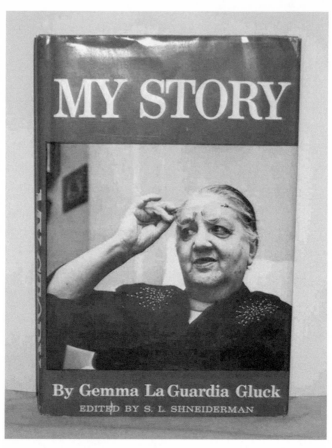

Book jacket for *My Story*, 1961. *Photo by Rochelle G. Saidel.*

8

Famous Names in the Camp

AMONG THE PRISONERS in Ravensbrück were wives, mothers, and sisters of the most prominent families of Europe—women like Madame Sarussel, wife of the mayor of Tunis; Madame Winkelkompes, wife of the mayor of Cologne, whose husband had been poisoned at a dinner given by Hitler; Madame Renée Sintensis, a noted Berlin sculptress; Madame Birgit Nissen from Oslo, once a delegate from Norway at the Geneva Disarmament Conference.

Madame Sophie Henschel, a member of a noted Austrian aristocratic family of Wurmbrandt, attracted everybody's attention. She was pretty and well dressed, and worked as a designer in the dressmaking shop. She had visited America before the war and spoke English perfectly. After the liberation, when I lived for a while in Berlin, she came to visit me and offered her help.

There was the Austrian Countess Josephine Ptacikova, who had a castle in Brunn called Schloss Stürtz, and had possessed jewels valued at seven and a half million crowns. Her castle and jewels were all confiscated by the Gestapo, and the countess died in the gas chamber after she became blind from the bad nourishment.

Also there was Madame Lelong, wife of a French general of the Colonial Army, who was a fine violinist and with whom I often talked about music.

Countess Lilly de Raubuteau was a relative of the Danish queen. She, her husband, and their four sons had lived in a castle in the vicinity of Paris. One evening French people came to the castle to ask for her help; when they received the assistance they had requested, they suddenly revealed themselves as the Gestapo in disguise. The family was scattered in different concentration camps. Madame Raubuteau was made to do very hard labor outdoors, loading cars. Then they put her on the sewing machines. She wasn't accustomed to work and she was sometimes whipped. The food was insufficient for her, and she was always hungry. Her husband was shot, but she and her four sons came out of this ordeal alive.

Madame Henry, the wife of the French ambassador to Ankara, was in Ravensbrück. So was Frau Wenzel, seventy years old, who owned fourteen estates and belonged to one of the richest families in Germany.

Frau Kantor was the wife of an Austrian banker, who had committed suicide in Vienna when *Anschluss*[1] came to Austria. I was very fond of Mrs. Kantor, who worked very hard to create a bit of social life in that terrible atmosphere. She organized Sunday concerts among the prisoners. I always managed to go to her block on Sunday afternoons. Imagine what it meant to all of us to be in a filthy, crowded block instead of in a beautifully decorated theater, looking at an emaciated prisoner instead of a prima donna in an evening gown. To see the singer

---

1. *Anschluss,* literally "union," is the term for the German annexation of Austria on March 13, 1938, without Austrian resistance.

we had to stretch our necks to find her sitting on the top of a three-decker bed. But we listened attentively to the wonderful melodies of Gounod's "Ave Maria" or Puccini's "Madame Butterfly." Most of the singers were French.

I was told that at Christmastime in other years no celebrations had been allowed and no presents permitted for the children in the camp. But in 1944, when I was there, Frau Kantor worked especially hard and got permission to have a Christmas tree made for the children. All blocks were allowed to contribute. How thrilling it was to see what beautiful things were made out of rags—dolls, dresses, aprons. Sketches were drawn by artists. Our block made balls, and so on. What ingenuity worked with the heart to make these children happy.

There was a young Czechoslovakian architect at the camp. She was employed in the camp's printing office. I asked her to draw picture books for the younger children. I dictated to her the story of "Little Red Riding Hood" and the story of "Cinderella." She printed the letters and illustrated the little books. This was our grand gift to the children, who enjoyed them tremendously.

At the beginning of April 1945, the energetic Mrs. Kantor was so happy that the end of the nightmare was approaching. She always kept saying to me: "Oh, Gemma, can you believe that we all shall be soon out of these tortures and saved, each prisoner going to her home and country?" About a week later she was carried to the hospital—she had caught typhoid fever. I left her on the 15th of April, when her condition was very serious. Later I asked other prisoners what had become of Mrs. Kantor, or Franzi, as we all called her, and they told me that she had died. She, the woman who was counting the days until freedom, remained there forever.

Also at the camp were Frau Sigrid Sailand, a Norwegian recitalist; Countess Lan[c]koronska, from Poland, and the Buchner family from Leipzig. The Buchners, a husband, wife, and daughter, had had a printing shop and turned out propaganda against fascism. All three were shot in the camp.

Another was Mlle. Geneviève de Gaulle, niece of General de Gaulle, a very young girl at that time.[2] Another Frenchwoman of note was Marie Claude Vaillant-Couturier, the widow of the French Communist leader and writer, Paul Vaillant-Couturier. She was active in the underground at Ravensbrück.

In Block Three was Frau Rosa Thälmann, wife of Ernst Thälmann, chief of the Communist party in Germany, who was executed by the Nazis in the Buchenwald camp. Also in the same block was the wife of another German Communist leader, Rosa Sefarowsky. One day Frau Sefarowsky was taken to the *Revier* for a gall-bladder operation. The S.S. surgeon, Dr. Percy Triete, performed the surgery successfully, and she recovered completely. A few weeks later, however, she was sent to the Oranienburg camp, where she was shot.

To the "famous" names of Block Three in Ravensbrück can also be added Olga Himmler, the sister of the Gestapo chief Heinrich Himmler. She was sent to Ravensbrück because she became involved in a love affair with a Polish officer in Warsaw. This was classified as *Bett-Politiker*.[3] I was told that Olga Himmler enjoyed exceptional favors and received special food during her stay at Ravensbrück. Then one day a Mercedes lim-

---

2. See Anthonioz (1999) for more information.

3. *Bett-Politiker* is related to the expression in English, "Politics makes strange bedfellows."

ousine arrived at the camp and a Nazi officer picked up Olga and took her away.

A late arrival in my block in Ravensbrück was Frau Hoffner, the wife of the Reichswehr general Hoffner, who was executed for his participation in the July 20, 1944, plot against Hitler.[4] The plotters had made an attempt on the life of Adolf Hitler, with the aim of overthrowing the Nazi regime and opening peace negotiations with the Allies. More than twenty top German officers who took part in the coup that failed were executed. Their wives were sent to Ravensbrück and dispersed into different blocks.

4. This most likely refers to the wife of Colonel General Erich Hoepner, executed by the Nazis on August 8, 1944.

9

The Bible Students

NOW I SHALL DESCRIBE briefly the Bible Students in the camp. They belonged to a religious sect that believes in the words of the bible as literal truth. I did not know of the existence of this sect before I came to Ravensbrück. I was told that it was founded by a certain Mr. Ford in North America and is known there under the name of Jehovah's Witnesses.[1] In Germany they were called Bible *Forscher* [researchers]. I had twelve members of the sect at my table.

Most of the Bible Scholars in Ravensbrück were simple, honest wives and mothers, a very hard-working lot. In this camp they were generally employed as servants, doing the heaviest labor. They told me they had been among the first prisoners at Ravensbrück and had been used for all kinds of construction jobs when the Nazis began to build the camp.

I admired these women for their strength of character. They had a staunch will and faith. They had been in prison for eight, ten, or twelve years, right from the beginning of Hitler's regime in 1933, when members of their sect refused to answer or acknowledge the official Nazi greeting, *"Heil* Hitler."

Bible Students insisted on the right to remain neutral in po-

---

1. Charles Taze Russell, born in Pittsburgh, Pennsylvania, in 1852, founded the Jehovah's Witnesses. The German term is *Bibelforscher.*

litical matters and not to be forced to salute a power that had been created by man, not God. "Render unto Caesar the things that are Caesar's and to God the things that are His" was their credo. The authoritarian Nazi regime could not stand for such disobedience, and thousands of Bible Students were arrested and sent to the camps.

At one point the Gestapo had announced that any Bible Student who renounced his beliefs and signed a statement to that effect would be given his freedom and be persecuted no longer. It is difficult to believe, but it is true, that not one of them signed such a statement. They preferred to go on suffering and patiently waiting for the day of liberation.

In the early days at Ravensbrück the Bible Students had refused to stand at attention during roll call. They stated they would stand in that manner only before God and not before anyone else. For this they were confined to the *Straf Block* (punishment block). The next morning they were kicked out of the block and compelled by physical force to stand at attention for roll call.

The Bible Students constantly tried to convert the other inmates of the camp to their faith. Even under the terrible conditions of life in Ravensbrück they showed themselves to be fanatics, having no tolerance for any religion other than their own. When Polish nuns arrived in Ravensbrück in 1944, the Bible Students showed open hostility to them. They wanted to burn the nuns' rosaries, which they called "tools of the devil."

10

The Punishment Block

FOR ANY INSIGNIFICANT INFRACTION one could be thrown into the punishment block. I knew an English lady who was unfortunate enough at a bed inspection to have the overseer find an English bible under the mattress. For this she received one month of suffering; she was thrown into the punishment block.

There was a German actress in our block who had written a letter addressed to some great person, expressing her opinions of Hitler. This letter she carried always with her, hidden in her clothes, since she had never found a chance to mail it to the addressee. As bad luck would have it, one morning in great haste to be ready for the roll call she left this letter under her pillow. It was found and she was thrown into the punishment block. She was tried and condemned to be shot, but at the last moment the commander postponed the execution since the letter had not been mailed. She was severely punished, and had to remain in the punishment block until the end. She would have been shot, but the liberation by the Russians saved her.

When I met her later, in Berlin, she let me read a copy of the letter with the same wording as the original one. It was really well written and she openly expressed her opinion against Hitler and his government, criticizing the brutal treatment of the prisoners and pointing out how the Nazis had destroyed art, music, culture, etc., and at the end she called Hitler "a fanatic devil."

Sad to say, there were many perverts among the women prisoners. When they were discovered they were sent to the punishment block and were given diverse, hard punishments, but I was told these women bore all their hardships well, as there they found more of their kind. Those who were found smoking or stealing were also put into this block.

The girls who worked in the kitchen of the S.S. officers' mess had many opportunities to steal pieces of meat, vegetables, fruits, delicacies, which the poor prisoners never saw. Some traded the food with other prisoners who worked in the storerooms where were kept the shoes, dresses, coats, and underwear that were taken away from the well-dressed prisoners on their arrival. Many of these expensive, lovely fur coats, dresses, and other items were things that belonged to poor prisoners who died or were sent to the gas chambers.

It was said that the nicest clothes came from the French women and from the Jewish ladies who were killed in Poland and whose clothing was sent to Ravensbrück to be sorted out. From Poland they brought freight cars full of furniture, typewriters, and pianos. Beautiful and valuable jewels were also taken from the prisoners.

We were all treated badly, but these poor French and Jewish women were brutally treated and misused. The women who were sent into the French and Jewish blocks had to work from early morning until night doing outside work, digging, making roads, building homes, cutting wood, in all kinds of weather. They were compelled to sing loudly when going to work early in the morning and when returning in the evening to their blocks. The walk was from half an hour to one hour long. The prisoners of the punishment block had to join the others in the above-mentioned work.

To distinguish the prisoners of the punishment block from the others, the Nazis cropped the women's hair so that if they tried to escape, their cropped hair would make them much more conspicuous and easier to catch. Toward the end of the war the S.S. officers decided that the next thing they would do to differentiate these prisoners from the others would be to pull out two front teeth, but thank God they didn't have time to do this, as the Russians were already approaching.

In desperation many of these women ran away. A very few succeeded. The ones that were caught received a terrible flogging of twenty-five blows with a leather whip every week for three weeks. The prisoner was stripped naked, had to lie on a board, and count every stroke she received. Sometimes she was stupefied and forgot to count, other times the great pain kept her from counting, and then she would get extra blows. After receiving these twenty-five blows the blood poured from all parts of her body and the pain suffered in the second and third weeks, when these blows came on top of the wounds, can hardly be imagined. Fellow prisoners administered the beatings for an extra portion of bread. Many women died of these blows, as the kidneys were often beaten out.

Dr. Gertrud Luckner personally knows of one case in Block Six where a woman who had been nearly four years in the camp was suddenly called and given a beating, which caused her death. She was brought to the concentration camp because she had been the mistress of a Pole.

The camp was surrounded by heavy electric wire and there was no chance of escape. Once two women tried to squeeze through the wire and were burned to a crisp. The dead bodies were kept on the wires for many days and we were ordered to walk past the blackened bodies. The camp overseers did this in order to wipe from our minds any thought of escape.

When I entered the camp, I thought to myself that someday I must describe all these horrors for the whole world to know how these women had suffered. I feared there were still some people who didn't believe all these unpleasant deeds to be true. Therefore, without arousing suspicion, I went everywhere and looked at all that was possible and listened to what was happening. If I had been caught I would have been severely punished. But as I was a special prisoner, I could walk around the camp, and therefore I saw and heard much, undetected. I purposely went to see a woman after her first beating. I'll never forget this scene and I didn't have the courage or strength to see her after her second and third beating.

The Jewish women had the worst and dirtiest work to do. Their block was the most unhealthy and dirty, with no electric lights. They were treated like animals and not like human beings.

On April 7, 1945, a week before I was sent away from Ravensbrück, thousands of big packages came from Canada to our camp. For the first time they were to be distributed among the Jewish women, too. As there were so many Jewish women in the camp, the commander said a trustworthy person must be appointed to be a witness and to hand out these packages, for which each individual was to sign her name. I was the person selected.

I began to give out these packages at 4 P.M., when there were a thousand hungry women standing in line. At 9 P.M. I was still handing out packages. I can't describe what a good feeling it was for me to be present at that scene, which I never want to forget. Some looked at me with such loving and grateful eyes, as if they couldn't believe what they saw. I tried to smile at each of them, as it wasn't permitted to speak to them, and with my smile I wished to encourage each of them to be brave and patient. At times I thought my heart would burst within me to see these women in such condition, ill, thin, dressed in rags, some were like walking skeletons, some the shadows of beautiful women, some so weak that when I handed them the five-pound packages they fell to the ground.

For the first time since I was in Ravensbrück I forgot myself, but thank God, I was not punished. In my Block Two there was a woman prisoner who also sat at my table. She wore the Jewish sign [yellow triangle] on her arm but she insisted that she was a Christian and that she had to wear this sign on account of her husband. She went from one office to another telling them that she was a Christian,[1] and in this manner she got rid of the sign. I also had the yellow stripe on top of my political sign [red triangle], as my husband was a Jew. She once came to me, saying: "Why do you wear this disgusting sign? Go and get rid of it as I have done." I answered her: "I'm wearing this yellow stripe because of my husband, and as I have been married for thirty-six years to such a good Jewish husband, I am proud to wear their sign."[2]

The argument was finished and nobody would have men-

---

1. The typed manuscript adds here: "and that she had to wear this sign on account of her husband" (manuscript pages 64–64a, ME 202, MM 28, LBI).

2. Generally Jewish political prisoners wore a red triangle pointed downward and a yellow triangle pointed upward, forming a Star of David. Nazi law defined Gemma as Jewish because her mother was Jewish; her designation was not just because of her husband.

tioned it again, but how great was my surprise when, as I was distributing the packages, I saw this woman standing in line among the Jewish women, waiting for a package. By my side stood the chief superintendent, Frau Binz. On my other side was the chief camp officer of custody, and before me was another woman prisoner from Vienna, who had been appointed chief of the camp police. Nevertheless, I forgot myself when I saw this woman coming forward to get a package.

In a nervous voice I shouted: "You impertinent woman. You say you are not Jewish, then what do you want here? If you say you are a Christian, then why will you cheat one of these poor Jewish women by taking a package away from her?" The superintendent heard me and said: "What has happened here?" in her shrill voice. I stood at attention at once and asked to be forgiven but continued: "Even if I am in a camp, I can't bear to see this unjust thing."

The superintendent was kind toward me and told me to explain what the matter was. Then I explained it all to her. The superintendent then said to me: "44,139, I'm glad you told me of this. I will attend to the matter." I became fearful at once of what would happen. But the officer merely called the woman into her office, looked up her records, and verified the fact of her being married to a Jew. She gave her one of the packages, but from then on the prisoner wore the yellow sign again.

11

The Political Meetings

THERE WERE POLITICAL MEETINGS inside Ravensbrück for the purpose of disseminating news of the war among the prisoners. They were held, of course, in great secrecy in all the camps. Not everyone participated in them, and those who made the arrangements were mostly the active anti-Nazis who had been imprisoned for their political activities.

The first political meetings at Ravensbrück were organized in 1940.[1] Three women of each nationality were chosen as leaders. They passed to each other whatever newspapers they could get hold of. They also managed to procure maps and made copies of them. After reading the war news they marked the maps to show what was happening. On Sundays small, quiet meetings were held among the prisoners who were interested. In their own languages the political leaders told the women what was going on in the outside world.

In our camp there was a broad street called "Main Street," where on Sundays we could go walking. Here we had continu-

---

1. More likely 1939. Gemma must have been told about these early activities, or Shneiderman added this from other sources, because she did not arrive until June 1944. From the camp's first days, the political prisoners organized themselves. For some examples of early political cultural resistance, see Saidel (2004, 41–52 and 60–62).

ally to walk up and down, never stopping or forming groups. The leaders always took this opportunity when they had their leisure time to speak to the others, telling them the news that they had found out and accumulated. The listeners as well as the leaders had to be very careful not to arouse suspicion, and by never pausing in their walking up and down they gave an impression of innocent exercise.

If perchance one of these meetings was discovered, great punishment would be enforced. Once twenty-five of these political women were arrested and put in a dark cell for six weeks. Another time several of these women received one year's sentence in the punishment block because they took part in a celebration of an anti-fascist incident. After the term of one year expired each woman received a beating of twenty-five blows. Notwithstanding that, these women still continued their political work with the greatest zeal.

I was told that in 1940 there was a woman prisoner who was a medical doctor who worked in the *Revier* (infirmary). This wonderful woman, who was an ardent anti-fascist, had such skill and shrewdness that she gained the trust of the S.S. doctors so that she could often act independently. She secretly helped sick women who were not allowed to be treated, and cured many of them.

When the prisoners were first brought to Ravensbrück, and were taken to the baths, they were robbed of all their possessions and also of any kind of medicine. I also was robbed of my heart medicament. The woman doctor worked with the prisoners employed in these baths. The employees took away the medicines from the prisoners and instead of handing them over to the S.S. officers, gave them directly to the woman doctor. Thus she was able to cure and help so many sick persons.

The political prisoners displayed great daring and courage. For instance, the list of those who were condemned to the gas chamber occasionally was destroyed. Many prisoners don't know to this day that they were sentenced to death and can thank their political leaders for saving their lives. These political prisoners also risked their own lives and undertook daily to make falsifications on the lists of the food allowances. They canceled out names in the work lists if their comrades happened to be ill. The name of an ill person would be exchanged for the name of a healthy person. When the prisoners were moved to other camps or to the execution places, these political prisoners hid many of them—some were even hidden among the corpses, which were lying in a cellar waiting to be cremated. On these occasions, when in the roll call one or more persons were missing, then the whole camp of fifty thousand prisoners was punished, and we all had to stand outside at attention for four to five hours in all kinds of weather.

12

The Rabbit Block

THE MOST HORRIFYING and shameful crimes at Ravens-brück were committed in the so-called Rabbit Block.[1] It was the barrack for the women who were used for experimental operations—like rabbits in a laboratory. The Nazis selected the most beautiful and healthy among the Polish girls, mostly in their teens, and sent them to the hospital for experiments.

I once visited the Rabbit Block. It was the best barrack in the camp. It looked like a real hospital, clean and orderly. The girls were given good beds. Doctors and nurses attended to the "patients."

I conversed with the Polish girls in German. Most of them had been arrested as members of the Catholic resistance movement. I found out that they did not know what they were there for. They thought they were really ill and were being treated by the doctors. Only later did it become known that the physicians were using them as guinea pigs in gruesome "experiments."

They were infected with various diseases in many different ways. Infectious materials and broken glass were inserted into open wounds, and when they started to run high fevers, the

1. For descriptions by Polish prisoners, see Póltawska (1964), and Symonowicz (1970).

doctors tested new drugs on them. They were placed into decompression chambers to test the limits of human capacity to withstand high altitudes, and they were submerged in freezing water to "study" human resistance to low temperatures. The girls were also used in abominable sterilization experiments designed to reduce the population of conquered lands.[2]

Then there were the "operations" performed on them by the Nazi surgeons. Some had muscles cut away or bones amputated in attempts to transplant them. A certain Professor [Karl] Gebhardt was often mentioned as the "outstanding" surgeon of these diabolical operations.

Dr. K. F. Gebhardt was one of Hitler's personal physicians. He was director of the sanatorium in Hohenlychen, situated about fifteen miles from Ravensbrück, which had been transformed into a big military hospital. Dr. Gebhardt used to come to Ravensbrück surrounded by a group of young doctors and immediately afterward their victims would be herded into the *Revier* by the S.S. overseers.

The doctors sometimes conducted their surgical operations without bothering to administer anesthesia. They sliced out muscles and amputated limbs, which were wrapped in linen and shipped to Hohenlychen. Thus this hospital for wounded Nazi officers always had a fresh supply of any parts of the human anatomy that could possibly be transplanted.

I did not visit the girls again, but later we heard about a

2. The high altitude and freezing experiments were done in Dachau, not Ravensbrück. Sterilizations were performed on Jewish, Gypsy, and other prisoners in Ravensbrück. Experiments on the legs of the seventy-four Polish women called "rabbits" simulated battlefield conditions to test methods to cure Nazi soldiers.

strike in the Polish block. The Polish overseer refused to deliver more girls for the experiments in the hospital. All the six hundred women in the Polish block were severely punished. They were deprived of food for four days and many of them collapsed.

Besides the Polish girls, one Ukrainian girl was used for the experiments in the hospital, as was a German woman who belonged to the Bible Students.

13

The Gas Chamber

IT WAS HIMMLER who ordered a gas chamber to be built at Ravensbrück in November 1944—for greater efficiency of extermination. The gas room resembled a bathroom and its door was labeled "Bathroom." The poor victims were told to undress, were given a piece of soap and a towel, and were led into the "showers." Instead of water, the gas was turned on.

Toward the end of the war, when the Nazis were murdering an incredible number of people, in their hurry they often took bodies out of the gas chamber that were not completely dead. The dead and half dead alike were thrown into lorries and carted off to the crematory. That was the end of millions of people, the majority of them Jews.[1]

What wisdom, talent, and fame became ashes here! What heartbreaking scenes there were of mothers torn from their children! One poor woman clung to her sweet three-year-old little girl when they ordered her to go to the "showers." Because she began to scream and beg them not to separate her from her child, the S.S. officers said: "Take your child, if you

1. This paragraph refers to the totality of the Holocaust and not only to Ravensbrück.

want it," and pushed the little girl in with the mother to be gassed.

My bed stood near a window in Block Two. As I could sleep little, I watched the grim flaming smoke pouring out of the chimneys of the crematory. And oh, the terrible odor. We could force our eyes shut, but we could not keep the stench of death away from our nostrils. When we were awakened at 4 A.M., the first thing we saw was the flaming smoke, the first thing we were aware of was the smell.

During Easter week in 1945 the crematory burned day and night: the frenzied Nazis wanted to get rid of as much "evidence" as they could. Just before the Russians arrived at Ravensbrück in April, the gas chamber itself was totally destroyed.

There was the "ice room" in Ravensbrück, where for some minor offense one had to stand barefooted for hours on the ice. For a severe punishment many prisoners were stripped of their clothes and thrown into the ice room. Is it any wonder that so many have come out permanently ill from these camps?

I knew a very nice, intelligent lady who was taken to Ravensbrück because she had been a member of a women's club that had worked against the Nazi government. One member of the club was a spy. The result was that the whole club was arrested, also the proprietor of the place where they met. When I last saw the lady at a reunion of the Ravensbrück prisoners in Berlin, she was nearly blind. Her punishment had consisted of having to lie down with a strong light reflector (which was hung from the ceiling) continually throwing its rays straight into her eyes. This torture was repeated several times.

It seems to me that the pleasure the Nazis took in tormenting innocent people should have merited punishment of the same kind. The S.S. should have been put into these camps for at least a year, and they should have been made to go through what the poor prisoners went through. After that, they should have been tried.[2]

2. Shneiderman made a correction to the proof page, leaving this short sentence. The uncorrected proof page said here: "After that the Nuremberg trials should have taken place and they should have been sentenced to death" (manuscript proof page 72, ME 202, MM 28, LBI).

~~~ 14 ~~~

Preparation for Evacuation

ONE AFTERNOON we received the order that the whole camp was to turn out for an inspection. We couldn't understand what this meant, as we had already stood for four hours for roll call that morning. This was about the second or third of April. Then a second order came that all prisoners must be barefooted. There was great excitement immediately. Each prisoner had a different opinion and there were agitated arguments as more than fifty thousand of us women went out to stand barefooted. We then heard that many doctors had come from Berlin to examine the prisoners to see who were sick, weak, or unable to walk.

As the Allies were approaching and the Nazis had to be ready to move quickly, only those prisoners who were strong and could walk would be selected for the march; those who wouldn't be able to walk in the long tramp, forty kilometers a day, would be shot down on the road. So one by one we had to walk in a line before those doctors, who watched our steps.

By this time I was looking very poorly, thin and pale. Besides, I was sixty-four years old. I was put aside with many others for the gas chamber. I can't describe my feelings in this sad moment. All from my block bowed their heads. I knew I was condemned to die, but I didn't care any more for myself, being so disheartened by everything. But when I thought of my dear ones, especially my baby grandchild, then oh, yes, I did want to live. My feeling at the first moment was as if I were going to choke, but of course I couldn't say anything. When we were dismissed and entered our respective blocks, I got a crying spell, my nerves broke down, and I began to scream like a little child, "I don't want to go through the crematory chimney."

The overseer of our block went at once to speak with [Fritz] Suhren, the commander of the camp, reminding him who I was. Because I was the sister of La Guardia, I was saved, but the others of my poor comrades were killed. The camp personnel director told me afterward that I was kept from the gas chamber because they were fearful that some harm would come to the Germans in New York in reprisal.

~❦~ 15 ~❦~

The Fate of Yolanda and Richard

DURING ALL THE TIME I was held prisoner at Ravens-brück, I never knew what fate had befallen the other members of my family. I thought of each one of them every night, praying that they were safe and unmolested. What irony that during those anxious nights my daughter and her baby were only one block away from me—right in Ravensbrück!

In August 1944, two months after my husband and I were arrested, the S.S. returned to our home in Budapest and arrested my daughter Yolanda Denes, her husband, and their five-month-old son, Richard. Yolanda and little Richard were shipped to Ravensbrück. Yolanda had been told that I had requested that she be brought to me. She was put into solitary confinement with her child in a cell that was just on the other side of Block One. Of course she never saw or spoke to the other prisoners.

Sometimes at night she was allowed to take a walk with a guard within the grounds to air the child. But she was told nothing of my whereabouts, and knew nothing that went on outside of her cell walls. She had nothing to do but to concern herself with the child whose strength was waning from the poor diet.

I was given a hint of this late in the spring of 1945 by another prisoner who worked in the personnel office. This young lady told me that she had seen a record of a Hungarian woman and her small son being kept incommunicado in the camp, and that from the description she thought it was my daughter. Of course I simply did not want to believe that Yolanda was in this dreadful place until I was forced to do so by proof.

I saw the proof shortly after the Canadian Red Cross packages were distributed to the Jewish prisoners. It was on the day that we learned that President Roosevelt had died.[1] Our hearts were heavy at the news—a real friend had died. The same young lady, who had given me the hint that Yolanda was there, came to see me in great excitement.

"Auntie," she said to me, "I have something to show you, but if you talk about it to anyone I'll be thrown into the punishment block."

"Of course I promise to keep secret anything you tell me," I assured her.

"Here is the receipt for the Canadian package signed by your daughter, Yolanda Denes," and she showed me the paper signed by my daughter's hand. I screamed, and fainted. Fortunately for me and the young woman, only another prisoner was in the barrack at the time. That night I could not sleep at all. This new knowledge kept eating at my heart.

This torture didn't continue for long, thank God, as a few days later the commander, Suhren, sent for me and asked me some puzzling questions. "I am searching in the camp for a certain Mrs. La Guardia. Do you know her?"

I replied:

"If you are searching for Mrs. La Guardia, you won't find

1. President Franklin D. Roosevelt died on April 12, 1945.

her here. But I think, Commander, you are perhaps seeking for a certain Mrs. Gluck, born La Guardia. If that is the case, here I am," and I looked at him straight in the eyes.

"Oh, is that so? Well, let me ask you another question. Do you know among your Hungarian comrades a certain Mrs. Yolanda Denes?"

"Yes," I replied. "Yolanda Denes is my daughter." But now came the moment that I had to play a part in an act and be as sly as they were and lie to them in order not to compromise the prisoner who had told me of my daughter. So I continued: "My daughter is not among the prisoners here, I hope."

"Where is she then?"

"I really don't know where she is now. I left her on the 7th of June, 1944, in Budapest at my home, and I do hope she's still there."

He then changed the subject. "Are you ill? You look very feeble. What complaints do you have about the food?"

I knew that this was a trick often used by them to get the prisoners to complain about something and afterward punish them for speaking against the camp.

So I replied:

"Commander, in the name of thousands of the prisoners I can tell you they are all very hungry, especially those who are working twelve hours a day, but I do not complain on account of food. This, Commander, you will never hear from me, but if you'll permit me to speak, I could and would complain of something else."

He became excited and very anxious, and said: "Speak."

Gathering all my courage, I said: "I complain that a woman who has been happily married thirty-six years should be suddenly snatched away from her husband and that for one year she hears nothing of him, doesn't even know where he is. I demand to know my husband's whereabouts and that you allow me to write to him."

I saw that he was a little embarrassed, and if he spoke the truth I really don't know, but he replied:

"Your husband is still in Mauthausen and I'll give him permission to write to you."

Then he dismissed me and immediately had my daughter called into his office and went through the same routine with her, asking:

"Do you know a certain Mrs. Gluck?"

My daughter answered:

"That is my mother whom I am waiting nine months to see. I was told that I was brought here because my mother asked for me."

"Well," he answered, "you'll see your mother soon."

On the afternoon of April 14, 1945, he brought us together. When my daughter saw me, she took a few steps backward. Afterward she told me she was frightened at my appearance. I looked so pale and ill and had lost forty-four pounds. She told me afterward: "Mother, you resembled a corpse." When I saw my daughter, I exclaimed: "Yolly," and wanted to run to her, but at once I remembered that I was a prisoner and stood at attention before the commander.

"Embrace your daughter," he said. "You are free, and now can stay together." I couldn't believe this happiness, and asked him if we would be with the International Red Cross. "No," he replied, "you are both going to Berlin tomorrow, escorted by a superintendent."

Oh, I was thunderstruck. Again my heart received such a blow, and a great fear came over me. Berlin—that word made me tremble. What would they do to us there? He saw what my thoughts were, and said: "Don't fear, you are not going to stay in Germany. Where you both will go I don't know. You are hostages and will be exchanged for some other prisoners."

Thus it happened that on April 15, 1945, at half past three in the morning, in pitch darkness, we were taken away from Ravensbrück.

I saw little Richard, my grandson, in my daughter's arms for the first time in nine months. He was now fourteen months old. His head was wobbly and he couldn't sit up. He had no teeth and couldn't grasp anything in his hands.

The cell where Yolanda and little Richard were placed on their arrival in Ravensbrück had only a single small window high up on the wall. The child was constantly looking up toward the bit of light that came into the dark dungeon. After a while he got the habit of holding his head tilted backward with his eyelids drooping. Little Richie was limp like a rag doll or a two-month-old baby. My first thought was: "Where am I going to bury this baby? He won't live."

~~16~~

The Last Days of the Third Reich

THERE WAS A LARGE DOUBLE GATE through which we had to go to the outside world. It was an everyday occurrence that a prisoner was told she was free and, with a full heart, was taken past that gate. Then, unexpectedly from behind, as she was walking toward freedom, there was a blast and she was shot down. So imagine our feelings. I looked suspiciously around, but we were safe, and we were allowed to walk out of the gate of hell.

We traveled by train in a second-class compartment to Berlin. Great was our surprise when the superintendent brought us to the notorious prison of the Gestapo in Prince Albert Strasse. Here we three were put into a cold room in a basement in solitary confinement. If we hadn't had the packages which we received in Ravensbrück from Canada, we would have been without food. Every night there were air raids.

On our first night in Berlin the Nazis notified us that when we heard the alarm we should go down to the shelter. Not knowing just where it was, we followed the crowd down the stairs. When I entered I stood astonished; it was like entering a drawing room, it was so beautifully furnished, full of elegance and pomp. We were just going to take our places when an S.S.

officer came and said: "Oh, no, this is not where you are staying. You are prisoners; come along," and they took us into a room which was full of water and gas pipes and electricity installations. There was a place for only one chair.

I was so frightened to be in there, as it would be terribly dangerous if a bomb struck it. I begged them to let us stay in our room, as in my opinion it was much safer. Outside of their luxurious dugout was a sort of hall where all the dogs were tied. I told the officer that I should feel much safer if they would let us stay where these dogs were, but he refused. We were kept in this room with the pipes every night. Once a bomb struck in the vicinity and some of the wall fell down. We were so frightened that we ran out, but they sent us back in again.

One evening I was sitting on the chair with Richard in my arms, my daughter standing nearby. Two S.S. officers came in out of curiosity, looked at my little grandson, and said: "Are you going to be such a diplomat as your great uncle?" I looked at them without speaking a word.

We had been confined five days in that damp, cold room in the basement with only one small, narrow cot where all three of us had to sleep. We had had nothing warm to eat or drink, and cleanliness for the baby was impossible. If my daughter or I had to go to the bathroom, we had to have a guard with us. In fact, we were treated like slaves. Where was our freedom?

I got quite angry, and asked to speak with any officer. When he came, I said: "Look here, please explain this treatment to us. The commander in Ravensbrück said we were free. Do you call this freedom? My daughter has kept her baby alive nine months in a cell. Now I'm not going to have this child get ill here. We can't even wash it properly."

"Don't worry," he said, "in two hours you will not be here."

We were again anxious as to what was going to happen to us and where our next stop would be. And again a surprise was waiting for us. They took us to another prison in Kaiserdamm, in Charlottenburg.

I didn't care any more what they did with us, but I did thank God that we were out of the Gestapo's prison. After the liberation of Berlin a German magazine published an article describing an incident in the prison.[1] On November 15, 1945, four graves had been opened in the cellar where 300 corpses were lying, thrown one on top of another.

It seems that at the last minute before the Russians entered Berlin all the people found in this prison were shot, so that nobody was able to tell what had happened within those walls. Not only were the prisoners shot but also the Nazi guards and S.S. officers. They killed them all so that the walls of the prison would be silent forever. This prison had served as a redistribution center for prisoners who were sent to Majdanek, Belsen, Mauthausen, Auschwitz, and Dachau. Here was the first station of their tortures. At the top of the Gestapo prison was Himmler's office. The cells for the prisoners were eight steps long, three steps wide, and into each one were crammed fifteen to twenty prisoners.

We were told at the Kaiserdamm prison that we would be kept only a few days as we were to be exchanged for some other

---

1. At the end of this sentence Shneiderman deleted from the page proof: "calling it 'The House of Terror' " (manuscript proof page 82, LBI). Today this site of the Gestapo headquarters houses the Topography of Terror memorial museum.

important prisoners. The few days passed—and the Russians burst into Berlin. The Nazis fought back fiercely and, even a few days before the end, Hitler spoke to the population of a Nazi victory, when he as well as all the Germans knew the end was coming for them. We spent the night and day in the prison's air-raid shelter.

A couple of days passed with terrifying nights of excitement. When everything became hopeless for the Nazis and they were trying to save their lives, they finally threw open the prison doors and we were all freed.

May God forgive me, but at that tremendous moment I rather would have remained within the prison walls than to get our freedom in such a manner. I begged the various overseers, the manager, to give me an address of the Red Cross or of some charitable society, a home of protection, as we had never been in Berlin and didn't know anyone, had no money, no credentials (the Gestapo had taken all away from us). Fortunately we knew the language, which was all we possessed, but these people remained cruel until the last minute and refused to give us any information or to help us in any way. They told us that we should be happy that we were free.

I must confess that, ironically, this was the worst moment of my imprisonment—we were free and we did not know where to go. Bombs were falling above our heads, the great noise of combat thundered around us, houses were burning. I pulled myself together and told my daughter to take up our bags and stand outside the prison doors and wait. "Where are you going?" she asked, terrified. I took little Richard in my arms and said: "I'm going where God will lead me," and began to run through the streets, wherever the road was clear.

In this excited and frightened state I arrived at the Charlottenburg railway station, where the bombs were coming down in full force, in all directions. Here, from feebleness, fright, and exhaustion, I nearly fainted with the fourteen-month-old baby in my arms. A policeman saw us and came to our aid and led me to a public air-raid shelter. I thanked him and asked him, as he was so good, to help me further, as I didn't know the way and couldn't leave my grandson alone to go to get my daughter with her bags. I explained where she was.

The policeman went to get Yolanda, but on the way back he began to question her, asking why she was in prison. My daughter didn't want to mention her uncle's name, knowing that it might anger the policeman, and so she said that her husband was a Jew. This was enough. The policeman became wild, dropped the bags, and was going to leave my daughter all alone in the middle of an unfamiliar street. My poor child became greatly frightened as the bombs were dropping constantly and she didn't know where we were. She implored him to have pity and at least tell her or show her where her child and mother were. He finally agreed to do so and brought her to us, but on the way he screamed out loud to everyone that he had committed a terrible crime. He, a German policeman, had helped a woman who was married to a Jew!

When we were reunited again in the air-raid shelter, we remained there eleven days and nights in darkness, almost without any food. If it hadn't been for the poor, good-hearted people who now and then gave us a piece of bread or a bit of black coffee or soup, we would have starved.

In our weakened condition, we had to sit eleven days and nights on a hard bench. Someone brought us an old baby carriage for Richard to lie in. How thankful we were for this. The awful fighting continued outside. Cannon were blasting on the streets, bombers were whining over our heads. The house next to the shelter was hit by a bomb. The windows of the shelter were all broken. Every moment we thought we would be struck by a bomb and buried in that cellar, for we were just opposite the railway station where the great attacks were taking place.

17

The Russians Enter Berlin

ON MAY 1, 1945, the Russians conquered Berlin. White flags were hoisted, but we who were in the shelter did not dare to go out. When evening came, many Russian soldiers, shooting pistols into the air, forced their way into the dugout, frightening the people with their shouting and shooting. They were demanding watches and jewelry from everyone.

My daughter said: "What are we going to do, Mother? I'm scared." I told her to be quiet, to take her baby in her arms and not to worry, that when they came to us, I would think of something. Of course, I was very frightened myself, but we had no watches or jewelry of any kind, for the Gestapo had already robbed us.

When our turn came and they stood before us, I looked quietly at them and spoke calmly in German, explaining that we had been in a concentration camp and that the Gestapo had taken everything we had from us. They remained standing before us, hesitating as to what they should do, as if they wondered if I spoke the truth. Obeying an impulse, I said: "Please leave us alone. We are Americans." I did not know how they would take these words, and a great silence fell in the cellar. Everybody waited to see how the Russians would take this news and what would happen.

It was an exciting moment but a beautiful one, for all the occupants of the shelter were stupefied when they saw the whole lot of the Russians stand at attention and give us a military salute. They said in broken German: "America and Russia are friends," and walked away without disturbing anyone else.

I don't wish to exaggerate, but I am quite sure that my words saved all the people in our cellar, especially the women and girls, as in all the other shelters the pillaging was terrible and the Russian soldiers were violating girls and women of all ages, taking them by force, and this didn't happen in our shelter. Mothers who were hiding their daughters in our shelter came to thank me.[1]

On May 2, 1945, we came out of the shelter in an indescribable condition. I feared that my little grandson might become blind from the long darkness. He couldn't look at the light, his eyes were so weak and full of water. My daughter, looking at me, asked: "Mother, are you ill? You look so dreadful." I really believe that Baby and I wouldn't have lived much longer in that terrible dugout. My daughter also looked so weak and tired and yellow. Her hands were all sores, having had to do all the baby's washing without soap in cold water every day.

Well, we were out in the open air and light, but our troubles began again. We still didn't know where to go and were without money, among strangers. One family in the shelter invited us to come to their home. I confess I didn't like the looks of these people and didn't trust them, but I thought until I could

1. The anonymous work *A Woman in Berlin* (2005) details how the dire conditions affected women between April and June 1945 and especially addresses the issue of rape by Soviet soldiers.

decide what we should do, we had to accept any offer. At least we would have a place to put our bags and for the first night in weeks have a place to sleep. So, with forebodings, we went to the German home.

Upon entering their flat it took us only one hour to decide definitely that we must not stay. I observed that the family was very busy burning up books, pamphlets, etc. I wondered at their hurry in burning these up, and became curious. The first chance I got, when they were out of the room, I quickly looked over these books and saw they were about Hitler's government and all about the Gestapo. So I said to my daughter: "Here we shall not remain. Keep Baby in your arms and wait for me. I'll go out and try to find some other place to stay before the night sets in."

On the first day I was in the shelter I was told to go to the police station to acquire ration tickets. I went—with bombs flying in all directions—leaving my daughter and grandson in the shelter. The first question asked was where did I live? My home address? I innocently answered the truth: "In a shelter."

"That is no home address," the official answered, "you must register where you reside."

I became furious and said: "Give me a home and then I'll be able to register."

"No home, no ration tickets," he screamed. Defeated, I returned to the shelter. This scene came to my mind thirteen days later, and I said to myself, if we don't get a home we won't have any ration tickets, so for us the only thing to do is to get a room of any sort, anywhere, and be quick about it.

I recollected that among the people in our shelter there was a very nice old lady with her daughter who told me she had a boardinghouse nearby. I went to her, but she didn't want to accept anyone yet, saying: "You see for yourself all is upset here and I can't take anybody in, there are no windowpanes, the glass in the doors is also broken." Otherwise she said she would take us in as she had pity on us.

I saw she was a real lady and the room was small but so nice and clean. So I begged her not to refuse, as I was so desperate and didn't know what to do or where to go. I told her not to worry about payment, as my husband would settle all, and in case he was not alive, my brother would pay all my expenses. That the windows had no panes made no difference to me, especially as it was summer then. She kindly answered: "I'm not worrying about the money, and if you are contented with the room, I shall paste cardboard on our windows, as windowpanes are not to be bought for any price."

Can you imagine what it is to have tears of joy? I ran to my daughter and told her the good news, that we finally would have a little room of our own. With lighter hearts we immediately went into the boardinghouse. Our room was clean, comfortable, and we had very kind people around us. That night I kept saying to my daughter: "We are sleeping in a real bed, can you believe it?"

Next morning I thought my first duty was to procure the ration tickets, now that we had a roof over us and I could give a home address. So I at once went to register for the coupons. At the office I had great trouble again as I had no papers to prove that we had just come out of a concentration camp. Anyone and everyone could say they had come out of a camp. The officials insisted that I give them some proof. Naturally having no papers, I had no proof. I told them I was registered at the

Kaiserdamm Prison. However, I very well knew that for two nights before we were freed I saw the S.S. officers were burning all papers and writings and destroying all the records before the arrival of the Russians. For this reason it's difficult to trace the prisoners, as in all camps and prisons the Nazi officials burned all the papers, registries, etc.

I saw I wasn't having any success in getting the ration coupons and I got quite desperate, as we had no food for the small baby or for ourselves and nothing could be bought without coupons. In my desperation I said: "Very well, don't give me the coupons but I'll see that my brother, La Guardia, mayor of New York, will know of this."

It was the first time I had used my brother's name to gain something. My brother Fiorello would have been surprised to see the effect of these words. Not only in America was he well known but also in Europe. Here in Germany they had taught the people that La Guardia was one of Germany's worst enemies. At my words everything changed. One employee ran here, another there, and in a few moments I had my coupons. Among the women employees who waited on me one seemed to pay particular attention to me.

Late that same evening I was very much surprised when the landlady told me that someone had come to see me. It was the woman employee with her daughter, bringing us fresh milk, biscuits, butter, jam, semolina, all things for Baby. What a kind and extraordinary gesture this was! They themselves didn't have much to eat.

I was so touched that from that moment on a great sympathy arose between us and it was this family with whom we finally lived in Berlin for one year. The woman's name was Frau

[Valley] Taroschowitz.[2] Every evening, after her hard day's work, she never went home directly but, for more than a month, in any kind of weather, she came to see us and asked if we needed anything and if she could do anything for us.

At the boardinghouse the proprietor and her daughter were also so kind, sharing their humble food with us. One evening, after we were there a week, a gentleman came to see us. It was the acting mayor of Charlottenburg, who had just heard that we were there and he came in his wife's name to invite us to be their guests. I thanked him and told him that I was very comfortable where I was and didn't accept his kind invitation.

I always had a private suspicion of everyone being a Nazi. I wondered: "Would my brother like me to accept this invitation?" He [the gentleman] went away, but after three or four days his young wife paid me a visit. She was really charming, and her kindness encouraged me, but I was still in doubt if I should accept her invitation. However, I knew that we could not stay much longer in the boardinghouse as there was so little room.

I thought of my grandson while she was tempting us by saying: "Baby can have what he needs and there are German Red Cross nurses in the building. You can have Baby examined by them." She described where we would live with them, in the City Hall, and we'd have a lovely healthy room with a large terrace on the Lietzensee. She pointed out that this would surely

2. The 1961 book says Jaroschowitz, but according to a typed July 15, 1945, letter from Gemma La Guardia Gluck to Fiorello La Guardia, her name was Valley Taroschowitz. Perhaps this was a misreading of a *T* in Gemma's handwritten memoir (LGW).

bring recovery of health for all three of us. Seeing that I was still undecided, she asked me why I wouldn't accept.

"Please don't be angry," I said, "but I must really know whose favors I would be accepting. I couldn't and wouldn't take a piece of bread from a Nazi family."

She smiled and said: "Then all is in order. I'll come with the auto to get you this afternoon. You see, my husband has just come out from the camp of Dachau. He was also a victim of the S.S., being imprisoned for four years."

The next day we went to stay with the acting mayor of Charlottenburg. And really, this large comfortable room, the fresh, pure lake air, the lovely terrace where we stayed the whole day, the better food, all this began to restore us from the hardships we had suffered. Daily I told them that my brother would repay their kindness. My thoughts were that living with a mayor would help me to reach the Americans when they came to Berlin and when my daughter and I would try to find our husbands.

18

Waiting for the Americans

IN THE FOLLOWING two or three weeks after the capitulation of Berlin a rumor was circulated that General Eisenhower was coming for a few days to Berlin and that from here he was returning to the United States. Well, I didn't lose time, thinking here was my opportunity, and I wrote a letter to the general, asking him only to inform my brother that we were alive and to tell him our whereabouts. I felt quite sure that the acting mayor of Charlottenburg would be in a position to see that the letter reached General Eisenhower. But I was disappointed. The mayor, his wife, and I drove to the general's residence but we were not allowed to see him nor were we permitted to send the letter to him. The mayor kept the letter, for I hoped that another occasion would come to appeal to some American officer.

Then I began to notice a strange thing about our hosts. Although we were given everything that we needed, still we were not allowed to go anywhere, even across the street to the park. It appeared in time that we were being kept, for some reason or other, as if we were *their* prisoners. I didn't like it, and told my daughter we should search for some private home to live in. I couldn't understand the mayor's intentions, for he never spoke to an American officer when he had a chance nor introduced us to anyone. I thought he really was doing everything for us for humanity's sake, that having himself suffered under the Nazis he understood our position, but I found out that he was not acting nobly but selfishly. He *was* keeping us as prisoners to use us as his tools.

For some reason or other the mayor didn't please the Russians, his position became uncertain, and the Russians had him removed from office. So, before he was discharged from his duties, he ran away with his wife. One hour before leaving he came and said to me: "Mrs. Gluck, pack up your things, take only what you need as we are escaping from here."

"What?" I exclaimed in excitement, but immediately came to my senses and said: "I'm very sorry to show our ingratitude in this manner, but I refuse to go away. We have suffered enough. I am an old woman, and my daughter with her little baby can't experience any more adventures. Why should we go with you? If you want to escape, do so. We will stay here in Berlin now until we find our husbands, or until my brother finds us. You have absolutely no right to take us along with you."

Then he became very angry and tried to frighten us by saying: "You don't know Berlin. Where will you go to live? Who will give you food?"

I simply replied: "Don't worry for us, think about yourself. We shall find a home."

Then I recalled that Frau Taroschowitz had already heard that something was wrong with the acting mayor, and had recently urged us that if things were not going right to pack up and go to her home even if it were midnight. "You'll live with us and we shall share our food with you," she said kindly. So I told the mayor that I was going to live with the Frau Taroschowitz family.

He and his wife became enraged and said furiously: "You must come with us, you have to help us, and without you (being an American) we can't reach the American zone."

Now, finally, I understood why he kept us so secluded from everyone and every place. Well, we didn't go with him but went to the Taroschowitz home. The acting mayor and his wife escaped in great secrecy. Nobody knew why or where they went; only after six or seven months we heard they were in a city which was in American territory.

From that day until we left Berlin we lived quietly with the Taroschowitz family, waiting to hear from our relatives. Frau Taroschowitz, learning that we were not even officially registered in Berlin, at once did so. Then she took me to an "Anti-Fascist" society that had been organized in Berlin to help all those who came out of the different concentration camps.

I discovered that the president, Maria Wiedmir, had been in Ravensbrück. I didn't know her there, since she wasn't in the same block as I had been. She had been a prisoner for eight years. Her husband had been shot, for he was a leader in the Communist party. She herself was active in the underground and did some of the most wonderful noble deeds. She had heard of me in Ravensbrück. From the first minute that she saw me in Berlin she was very kind to us three. She found some clothes for Baby and shoes for us. We also could buy potatoes and vegetables at very reasonable prices through the society. Later in the winter we could buy coal and wood. This was wonderful, indeed, for at that time in Berlin nothing could be bought on the market.

In this same society I made the acquaintance of a Hungarian gentleman, Mr. Vida, a journalist and poet, who had been in Dachau four years. He was the director of the radio in Charlottenburg. I heard a recital of a selection of poems he wrote at Dachau. They were so pathetic, so moving.

Mr. Vida arranged for me a broadcast interview in German about my experiences in Ravensbrück. On the program I asked that whoever knew the whereabouts of my husband and my daughter's husband [should] write to us. But, sad to say, we had no success.

In Berlin great excitement grew as the English troops began to arrive. Now, as Mr. Vida lived in the English zone and as we did not know where the American zone would be, he suggested that he would introduce me to the British general so as to contact the Americans. And this he could do for me as he personally knew the general.

The English general was rather stiff in the beginning. After the formal salutations I told the general that I wanted only his advice as to how I could get a letter into the hands of the American authorities, asking them to let my brother know that we were in Berlin.

The British general spoke very kindly. "Mrs. Gluck," he said, "give me your letter. It will be in the American headquarters this evening. But remember you must have patience for a few days, as the Americans have just arrived and are too busy to occupy themselves with private affairs. But I am convinced that you will hear from them."

I thanked him and went home with a lighter feeling, thinking that in some way or other my brother Fiorello would soon hear from us. I supposed that in a few days perhaps I would see some Americans who could notify him that we were in Berlin.

Can you imagine our surprise when early next morning all Fritsche Street, where we were living, was suddenly full of American jeeps with American officers? The Germans in our street couldn't understand what was happening or who was living here.

It must be that at the United States headquarters the news quickly spread that La Guardia's sister, niece, and grand-nephew were in Berlin, for besides several United States Army officers many war correspondents arrived. I had eight interviews that day with different newspaper reporters.

On the following morning at 2:30 A.M. a reporter from the Associated Press, Mr. Daniel DeLuce, awakened me.[1] That's American tempo for you! He had just learned about me from his colleagues. I must say that I was quite angry to be disturbed at that hour, but he was so apologetic and kind that I could not scold him. I told him my story as I had told the reporters the previous day, and added some extra facts.

On the following morning, at quite a decent hour, Mr. DeLuce appeared again, laden down with great overflowing boxes full of the most wonderful food and goodies. He told me that they were contributed by soldiers and correspondents who gave readily and generously when they heard the plight of the sister of a man they loved, Fiorello La Guardia. My grateful thanks mingled with my tears.

1. In 1944 Daniel DeLuce won the Pulitzer Prize for international reporting for his Associated Press series on Yugoslavia.

~ 19 ~

The Voice of Fiorello

I OWE MUCH GRATITUDE to a lady of the Mutual Broadcasting Company, Captain Kathryn Cochran Cravens, then of the United States Army and now of New York City.[1] She arranged to have broadcast in the United States an interview in which we spoke about Ravensbrück. My brother heard the broadcast in New York. I have always been enthusiastic about the invention of radio but at the moment Captain Cravens told me that I was going to speak with Fiorello I thought radio was a miraculous wonder.

Can you imagine what it meant to me? After having suffered so much, after not having spoken to my brother for over twenty years, they notified me that I would speak with my brother in a few minutes. We spoke for several minutes—at last my brother knew we were alive and where we were. I could now rest assured that in the future he would take care of us and do all in his power to get us to the United States.

I was so utterly helpless at that time, knowing neither the

---

1. The 1961 book used the name Katherine Craven, but Kathryn Cochran Cravens (1898–1991) is the correct name. A radio personality, actress, and novelist, she was the first woman accredited as a wartime radio correspondent and one of the first broadcasters from Berlin following the Allied victory in 1945.

country nor people. My daughter and I still knew nothing of our husbands, and we had lost all—home, possessions, clothing, certificates of birth and marriage. We had nothing. It is a bitter thing to have nothing in one's old age. One is almost too weary to start a new life. When I came out of Ravensbrück I thanked God that I was free and that I had come out of that hell. Then I was grateful for His having given my daughter and my grandson back to me. But in the months following, when I didn't know what to do, which way to go, those days were so bewildering that I would forget myself and often said: "What was the struggle to keep alive for?" But, thank God, these thoughts didn't last long, and I used the strong will, perseverance, and energy of the La Guardias to keep my head and spirits up.

I regained my courage completely when I heard my brother's voice in our broadcast.

"Hello, sister!" Fiorello said.

"Oh, Fiorello," I replied, "is it really you? I can't believe it!"

"No time for sentiments," he retorted in his brisk way. "Tell me what you want me to do, and I will do it."

When I told him we wanted to come to the United States, Fiorello answered: "All right, sister, but you must have patience. Things can't be arranged so quickly, and you know you must wait for your daughter's turn in the immigration quota, for I won't make any exceptions."

These were his words, and they were enough for me. When the whole population of New York City had trust in him, you can imagine the faith in him of his only sister. I became full of hope. Doesn't it sound rather ridiculous to hear that at my age I was ready to start a new life, full of illusions and hopes, and would have been the happiest woman in the world if my husband had been with me to start a new life in this great land of freedom?

Five months elapsed—and no news. Nothing happened. We were still in Berlin with absolutely no news from my husband or my daughter's husband. The one pleasure we experienced was that I received the first letter from my brother.[2] I can't describe this feeling—to hold a letter in your hand from somebody you love, whom you had never expected to see again.

Although the ocean divided us, I felt I still had someone left who would think of our future and take care of us, as I knew my brother's heart. The great darkness that surrounded our lives brightened up with my brother's letter.

2. For the full text of this letter, dated October 31, 1945, see the appendix, pages 141–44.

~~~20~~~

First Reunion of Camp "Graduates"

ON SEPTEMBER 9, 1945, the Anti-Fascist Society in Berlin held a memorial for the victims of fascism. The great spectacle took place in the Olympics Stadium at Neuköln. What a sight! Sixty thousand people were present, of all nationalities. They were the former inmates of all the various concentration camps. Such a moving scene as they gathered together, all sad, many ill, others crippled, many malformed, having lost either a leg, foot, or arm through the tortures they went through; each one of these people could write a book of his own sufferings. A lake could have been formed of all the tears that these sixty thousand prisoners had shed in their lives.

In this sports stadium, which is internationally famous, a huge empty space had two enormous urns with fire burning inside, in memory and respect to the dead—the victims of the Nazi atrocities. Chopin's "Funeral March" was played. In the procession a group represented every camp. Men and women carried beautiful wreaths of leaves and flowers, placing them before the urns. About a thousand wreaths were brought to honor the poor dead victims. At that time my daughter and I didn't know that our husbands were among these victims.

Some of the men in the procession wore their blue-striped uniforms of the prisons [concentration camps]. This recalled such sad memories that when I saw them I burst into tears, and it all came back to me how in Mauthausen my husband and I were compelled to wear these striped suits. A great orchestra played the "Overture Coriolina" and the "Leonore" by Beethoven. Then we heard an excellent choir sing some very sad songs that had been composed in the concentration camps. Among others a beautiful one was composed by Mr. Vida. Solemn speeches were made by the mayor and other distinguished persons of Berlin and by some of the ex-prisoners.

A wonderful poem written by a former prisoner was recited. It was such a sad verse that no one who heard it could have dry eyes. It was called "The Children's Shoes from Lublin." This poem was about an actual happening. Thousands of Jewish children had been gathered together in the Lublin concentration camp known as Majdanek. One day the children were told that they would be taken to see a football game. The poor innocent children rejoiced and went away with smiles on their faces and laughter. Where were they taken to? Nobody knew. All trace of them was lost until one day there came back to Lublin, not the children, but thousands of pairs of shoes, all sizes. The shoes came back, but the children had been taken to the gas chamber.

During the time I lived in Berlin some of the women who had been my comrades in Ravensbrück came to visit me. They told me about events that took place after Yolanda and I left. On April 28, 1945, the Russians were getting closer to the camp, so all the prisoners were given the command to be ready in half an hour to start for a march. It was the Gestapo's plan to move these thousands of women to a great munitions factory in the neighborhood and then to blow up the factory. But their ghastly plan failed, as the Russians took possession of the factory first.[1]

Nevertheless, the camp officials drove the women en masse across the country in order to destroy as much evidence in the camp as possible. Without food and without stops for sleep or rest, the women feebly dragged themselves on. They were compelled to throw away whatever rags or extra belongings they carried, as the weight became heavier and their bodies became feebler. Those poor ones who couldn't keep pace were shot and left along the road. The liberation by the Russians finally set these women free.

My friends further told me that when my daughter, her baby, and I were sent to Berlin, they all thought that we would surely be shot. Others thought that Commander Suhren planned to keep us in Berlin as hostages for himself. Long afterward I heard that he was caught and imprisoned by the Russians and later escaped from them.[2]

I saw as many of my former Ravensbrück friends who were now in Berlin as I could. I also met many men and women who had been in the other concentration camps. Their eyewitness accounts of horrifying experiences could be written into many volumes. Some of them have written their own personal histories.

---

1. For more information on Ravensbrück's last days and the death march, see Saidel (2004, 166–77).

2. Suhren testified in April-June 1946 at the Nuremberg trials conducted by the United States. He escaped before he was to be tried at the Ravensbrück tribunals, which were held in Hamburg by the British in late 1946 to 1948. He was recaptured in 1949, handed over to French authorities, and tried in Rastatt. He was sentenced to death and executed in June 1950.

We have by now all heard or read of the ruthless criminal actions committed by the Nazis, we know that millions of innocent people were viciously tortured and killed. Among those people were many noble, brave souls, who risked and gave their own lives to help others. It is that nobility of the human being that survives even in the face of bestial brutality which makes it possible to believe in God and the future of humanity.

Some of these concentration camp "graduates" that I met survived their ordeals and came through unmaimed except for physical tolls. Others, understandably, have lost faith in their fellow men and have had difficulty in adjusting themselves in the postwar world. Those happy people who have never had the stench of the "super-clean" concentration camps in their nostrils can now demonstrate their sympathy by showing some patience and tolerance.

We received tangible evidence of my brother Fiorello's concern about us when Mr. Carroll, at that time head of the American Red Cross in Paris, flew to Berlin to see me, bringing me some money and food.[3] He arranged for the Red Cross in Berlin to keep us supplied with condensed milk, porridge, chocolate, and fruit, which they did for two months. Little Richard gained weight and the roses started to come back to his cheeks. His soft little arms and legs started to get harder and to develop muscle.

---

3. Frederick Carroll was killed in a car accident in October 1945, according to a letter dated October 31, 1945, from Fiorello La Guardia to Gemma La Guardia Gluck (LGW). This was verified via e-mails to the editor of this edition from the American Red Cross in 2005.

~21~

The Tragic Death of My Husband

YOLANDA AND I kept anxiously asking everyone for some news of our respective husbands. We had no idea whether either one was alive. The Germans in the British sector of Berlin arranged for me to make a short speech on their radio, to ask if anyone listening in had any knowledge of my husband's whereabouts. As the name Gluck is so common, I received many letters, but they were all about the wrong Herman Gluck.

The bad news about my husband came to me in April 1946. Our German landlady saw a newspaper article about a Dr. Joseph Podlaha, a professor of medicine in Czechoslovakia who had also been a prisoner in Mauthausen. He was a witness at a trial held in Dachau, by an American military court, of sixty-one former overseers of the Mauthausen extermination camp.

Dr. Podlaha testified that he had witnessed the death of a Herman Gluck who was the brother-in-law of the former mayor of New York and director of the UNRRA [United Nations Relief and Rehabilitation Administration], Fiorello La Guardia. It seems that my husband developed some sort of abscess that required an operation, which Dr. Podlaha performed successfully. However, shortly afterward the hospital was relocated and all the Jewish prisoners were killed.

Dr. Podlaha wrote in reply to a letter I wrote beseeching all the information he could give me: "I am very sorry to write you, Mrs. Gluck, that your husband was indeed a victim of the Nazis. And it was upon the order of that beast of a camp commander, Franz Ziereis, that he had to die."

Later I heard an account of the sufferings of my husband from an old friend of ours in Budapest, Dr. Zoltan Klar, a physician by profession and a writer by avocation. He was also very active politically, and for some time was a member of the Budapest parliament.

Dr. Klar had courageously fought the Hungarian fascists with pen and sword. As one of the foremost fencers in Hungary, he had successfully fought many duels with political enemies and he was known as a modern Cyrano de Bergerac. Now Dr. Klar lives in New York. He edits a Hungarian language weekly, *Az Ember* (The Man), in which he continues his battles with Hungarian Nazis who escaped punishment and now live comfortably in the United States.

Dr. Klar was a prisoner in the Mauthausen camp at the time my husband was there. Thanks to his medical training, Dr. Klar was appointed head of the medical staff, which the Nazis recruited from among the prisoners for the hospital that was maintained principally to deceive visiting Red Cross delegations. The staff included more than two hundred well-known doctors, among them some of the most celebrated in the profession. Only five of them survived.

Dr. Klar secretly kept a record of all prisoners brought to Mauthausen. He told me he saw my husband frequently. Herman was quartered in a block among some of the privileged prisoners. Because of his relationship to my brother, Fiorello, the Germans kept him there for the purpose of a possible exchange for a valuable German prisoner.

Dr. Klar told me of the many conversations he had had with my husband. Herman always asked him if there were any letters from me. I wrote to him constantly, but it seems he never received my letters. Whenever new prisoners arrived from the outside world, my husband always inquired whether they had any news of his wife, daughter, and grandson.

For many years I had no knowledge of the exact circumstances of my husband's death. More detailed information about what had happened to Herman reached me on my eightieth birthday, April 24, 1961. It cast a pall of sadness on my reunion with some of my fellow Ravensbrück inmates with whom I spent that day.

On the occasion of my birthday, I received numerous gifts, messages and visits from friends and neighbors and even complete strangers. Some of the [visits] were from Ravensbrück survivors whose names I had lost with the passage of the years but who still remembered me.

Among those who called on me was Rabbi Isidore Selig Cohen, who had been spiritual leader of the Orthodox Jewish community in Budapest. It was not until 1959 that Rabbi Cohen was able to immigrate to America, where he settled in New York. He had spent many months at Mauthausen in Block Twenty-four, where the Nazis kept my husband among the prominent Hungarian Jews they were holding as hostages for possible political use.

The rabbi told me how the block had been thrown into panic in the early morning of January 1, 1945. An S.S. sergeant named Bokser, one of camp commandant Franz Ziereis' most bestial assistants, suddenly strode into the barracks. He was roaring drunk, apparently having come directly from the camp overseers' New Year's party. Hoarsely he shouted orders for all Jews to line up. The first to come forward was Dr. Leo Goldberger, who had been a well-known industrialist in Budapest. Bokser struck him to the floor with a single blow.

Suddenly, Rabbi Cohen recalled, Bokser seemed to recognize an individual familiar to him in the mass of people herded before him. It was my husband. The sergeant pointed to him and asked him to step out. Bokser made as if to shake hands with Herman, saying: "Servus, Herr Bürgermeister, how are things in New York?"—apparently an allusion to Herman's brother-in-law, Fiorello La Guardia. Without warning, Bokser seized Herman by the hand, hurled him to the floor, and trampled him until he lost consciousness. The Nazi beat up a dozen other men before he left Block Twenty-four that morning. The injured were taken to the *Revier,* where most of them died. Herman Gluck was one of these.

In the *Totenbuch* [list of deaths] recording Mauthausen's victims that was secretly kept by Dr. Klar, who attended my husband after the fatal beating, Herman's name appears under the date of January 6, 1945.

Concerning my daughter's husband we finally had word that he had died at Mauthausen—from starvation.

With the news of our husbands' deaths, half of our hopes died. We would never again live as we had lived in Budapest, never again would we feel the security of being with the heads of our families. Survival would always be up to us alone—with help from no one, unless we humbled ourselves to ask for it.

I must say that there were kind people all along the way, who helped us without our asking for it. Among them were Captain Joseph Shubow, the Jewish chaplain of the United States Army in Berlin, Captain Cravens of the army network, and Miss Emily Mikszto of the WAC [Women's Army Corps], who brought us food, goodies, cheer, and much-needed advice.[1]

Chaplain Shubow worked day and night helping Jews who were fortunate enough to be liberated from the concentration camps. In many ways he helped to rekindle the spark of humanity that was almost beaten out of many of the former prisoners' souls.

Every Wednesday evening he held a social for the DPs and the Jewish people in Berlin. On Friday evenings he held a ritual service. Some of us who had come out from the camps thought we wouldn't know how to live any more—how to act like civilized people, but the chaplain went among us, saw and understood.

After the Friday evening service every week he organized concerts. How that music soothed us and reminded us of how wonderful life used to be. And then he served sandwiches and coffee to his guests, who will long remember the awful pangs of constant hunger. Can you know what this small gesture of kindness meant?

Chaplain Shubow received many food and clothing packages from individuals and organizations in the United States. He distributed them generously and fairly among all. There were Jews in Berlin who escaped the camps by living "illegally"—hidden by Christian families. To these Christian fami-

1. Emily Mikszto married Hugh Salzberg after World War II and lived in New York, where she continued to stay in touch with Gemma.

lies who were in need Chaplain Shubow also gave assistance. Today he is the rabbi at Brookline, Massachusetts. That city must be happy to have such a good rabbi. God bless him and his family.[2]

2. After serving as a U.S. Army chaplain in World War II and postwar Berlin, Rabbi Joseph Shubow (1899–1969) was the rabbi of Temple Bnai Moshe in Boston. He was also a national vice president of the Zionist Organization of America.

~22~

My Return to New York City

IN THE SPRING of 1946 I received a letter from Fiorello, explaining that as head of UNRRA he preferred not to help his own flesh and blood first among the DPs.[1] That we would have to take our turn or, better still, he decided to get us transported to Denmark, from there to travel as private passengers to New York. The arrangements, such as visas and permits, were taking a great deal of time; naturally we were neither happy nor very comfortable in Berlin.

That summer he wrote that he would make an UNRRA survey throughout Europe and that he would see us in Denmark. Of course we were overjoyed.

I had had a strange dream, long before my imprisonment, of being taken to a headquarters somewhere and being confronted by five or six men in uniform. Someone said to me in my dream not to fear the men, for they were American officers. "How do I know they aren't the Gestapo in disguise?" I asked suspiciously. Whereupon one of the officers stepped forward

---

1. President Truman named La Guardia director general of the United Nations Relief and Rehabilitation Administration in March 1946. Funded mainly by the United States and Great Britain, UNRRA's mission was to provide emergency food relief and help to rehabilitate war-torn European countries. La Guardia resigned in December 1946.

with his hand extended, saying, "Mrs. Gluck, I am Major Thompson. Your brother sent me to help you in any way I can."

For some reason this dream made a deep impression on me and during my days at Ravensbrück, when I heard the hum of planes over the camp, I often wondered if my "Major Thompson" would come. I told some of my comrades in the camp about it and they, too, would say: "Here comes your Major Thompson."

The sequel to this dream occurred in July 1946, when my landlady announced that some Americans had come to the apartment to see me. I wasn't surprised by now at these visits, for my brother had communicated with the United States Army authorities in Berlin about me, and several officers, including an army doctor, had come to see me. But you can imagine how astounded I felt when one of the officers stepped forward and said: "Mrs. Gluck, I am Major Thompson. I shall be glad to help you in any way that I can." So, you see, Major Thompson did come to me. . . . And it was he who helped us to take our first steps toward leaving Germany.[2]

Fiorello arranged for us to be moved to Copenhagen, Denmark, to wait there for three months for all our visas to be put in order and then to embark on a ship for the United States.

There were many interviews and long waits in the United States consul's office and in the British authorities' office in Berlin before I obtained my American passport and military

2. A Western Union telegram, dated April 22, 1946, to Major R. N. Thompson, displacement officer, Berlin, from Fiorello La Guardia, says: "THANKS KEEP ME INFORMED CABLE PROPER TIME WHAT CITY DENMARK I CAN WIRE FUNDS GEMMA AVOID PUBLICITY LA GUARDIA" (LGW).

permits to travel for Yolanda and Richard. I had, of course, lost my American citizenship in 1908 when I married my Hungarian husband. His death—what a terrible price—restored my citizenship to me.

We embarked on our journey to Denmark in lorries with many other displaced persons. These huge British trucks took us to Bremen. It was May 1946, and the healing countryside was beautiful for us to see and to breathe after the ugliness of shattered Berlin. We spent a week at Bremen, waiting for further arrangements. Then we went to Hamburg by train.

We were told we would be met by a representative from the American legation on the station platform at Hamburg. As we stood waiting for him, huddled together with our few belongings, the train pulled away from the station. As we looked up at it we were tremendously surprised and honored to see at all the windows United States soldiers saluting us. In spite of our traveling so quietly, they had found out who we were. My eyes filled with tears. They were paying honor to my brother, Fiorello La Guardia.

The American consulates and the Danish Red Cross outdid themselves in kindness and consideration in getting us out of Germany and to Denmark. I shall always be grateful to the many gracious individuals who greeted us, arranged for our meals, lodging, and transportation, and treated us like human beings.

The American legation in Copenhagen arranged for us to stay at a charming little boardinghouse at Hellerup. [It had] excellent food, kindly people, pleasant surroundings, and— best of all—a sunny garden for little Richard to play in.

So we settled down to wait. And the waiting started to stretch on and on, as my daughter's Hungarian nationality was the subject of much international discussion and arrangements. We now needed a super supply of patience. We were so close to that heaven—the U.S.A.—and yet so far away, across yards and yards of red tape.

Meanwhile, we enjoyed the lovely little heaven of Denmark. We slowly started to get about, à la tourists. We saw the King's Palace, the Museum of Art, the Royal Theater, the ballet.

In September 1946, the Danish newspapers blossomed out with big headlines about my brother. He was touring Europe as head of UNRRA, visiting each nation that was receiving aid—and he was really coming to Copenhagen! Tirelessly, never resting, he pushed on from country to country, sizing up the economic situation in each one.

Early one morning I was called to the phone. It was Fiorello speaking! He was already in Copenhagen and was calling to tell me that he would be at my boardinghouse at noon. How excited I became! I had not seen him for twenty years. I could hardly contain my tears of joy.

Characteristically, when he arrived he was unsentimental, brisk, and businesslike. He informed us that he was doing all within his power to get us to the United States, but that we would simply have to wait our turn in the visa quotas. He could not treat us as if we were any more important than the thousands of other displaced persons who were waiting to get to America.

At that time the Copenhagen Fair was going on and my brother was invited to speak at a special meeting held at the fair. He took me to hear the speech. I was so proud of him—everyone paid such high honors to him. I had the pleasure of meeting Lady and Sir John B. Orr, who were also at the fair.[3] For a

3. Lord John Boyd Orr (1880–1971) won the Nobel Peace Prize in 1949. Born in Scotland, he was a physician and director-general of the Food

moment I felt as if I were back in the grand old days when Fiorello escorted me about to his social engagements in New York when I came to visit him as a young woman.

It truly did my heart good to have Fiorello with us for those few days in Denmark. I had the feeling of a shipwrecked person who clings to a strong mast. The mast was my brother, who held all my hopes for the future.

When he left, flying away in a great plane, life felt empty again. The winter months passed by slowly, and then came spring. On the first of May, 1947, came a letter from my brother—all was in order at last![4] And seven days later we were notified that passage was available on a Liberty ship leaving in two days. We were overjoyed. Everyone at the boardinghouse was so kind. They gave us a gala farewell with a dinner and gifts.

The trip was a pleasant one. We arrived in New York on May 19. My brother was in Canada on that day. His wife, Marie, came to greet us at the pier and made arrangements for us to stay in an apartment in Brooklyn.

---

and Agriculture Organization of the United Nations. In 1946 he set up an International Emergency Food Council to meet the postwar food crisis. He was also president of the National Peace Council and World Union of Peace Organizations.

4. See appendix, page 148, for the letter from Fiorello to Gemma dated April 19, 1947. Many letters and documents provide evidence that Fiorello used high-level contacts to finally bring Gemma and her family to the United States. For example, a letter dated May 8, 1945, from Josiah Marvel, Jr., the chief of mission for the American embassy in Copenhagen, informed Fiorello that arrangements had been made for Gemma's voyage. According to his letter to Fiorello of May 12, 1947, Emmet McCormack, treasurer of the Moore-McCormack Lines, was involved in arranging passage on one of his company's ships, the SS *Mormacpenn* (LGW).

When I saw Fiorello a few days later my heart almost stood still. He had become so thin and pale. I could see that he was a very sick man. Almost immediately, he entered a hospital, but as nothing could be done for him, he was permitted to return to his home.

This was the final measure of suffering I had to bear—to watch my beloved brother grow weaker and weaker. He did not know that he had a fatal disease and that these were his last days. His wife had skillfully hidden the truth from him. He talked optimistically to me of getting a nice little home for me and Yolanda and Richard. He reassured me as to Richard's future; he would see to it that the little boy would have a good education. He had a child specialist come in to give Richard a thorough examination. The doctor pronounced him healthy and well developed in spite of his babyhood in a concentration camp.

I was permitted to see less and less of my brother, and on September 20 he passed away. The grief of New York City was made known to his family in many ways. We were all touched by the tributes to him, showing the city's love and devotion to the Little Flower. Not only New York but the whole country and the world mourned him. I received articles from newspapers in the Netherlands, Denmark, Italy, Germany—all regretting the loss of this man who truly lived for others.

All of Fiorello's plans for us vanished with his death. Again I was left alone with my daughter and her little son. But at least we were in the land of opportunity, the land of the free. There was hope here.

This is the story of my life—of the youth that I shared with Fiorello and of the concentration camp imprisonment that I experienced with millions of other victims of the Nazis.

Because fate gave me such a famous brother, my life has been full of pride and great happiness, but also of suffering and heartbreak. Being a La Guardia was the reason for my incarceration in Mauthausen and in Ravensbrück, but ultimately the name La Guardia saved my life and those of my daughter and grandson.

I hope that this memoir will remind those people who too easily forget what happens when fear is the ruler of the land, and when men become less than men.

Epilogue

WHEN GEMMA LA GUARDIA GLUCK celebrated her eightieth birthday at her Long Island City apartment in Queens, New York, in April 1961, she announced to a reporter for the *New York Times* that her memoir, *My Story*, would be published that fall. "She unfolded a ninety-page memoir of her experiences in Ravensbrück that she wrote shortly after she was released at the end of the war," according to the reporter. "A paragraph referring to Mayor La Guardia's arrival in Copenhagen said: 'Characteristically, when he arrived he was unsentimental, brisk and businesslike. He informed us he was doing all within his power to get us to the United States but that we would simply have to wait our turn in the visa quotas.' Her memoir is included in testimony to be offered against Eichmann. It will be published here in September as *My Story*" (*New York Times* 1961).[1]

The guests at Gemma's birthday party, listed in the article, included another Ravensbrück survivor, old friends, her daughters Yolanda and Irene, and her four grandchildren. Dr. Zoltan Klar, who was with Gemma's husband Herman in Mau-

---

1. At Yad Vashem and the Israel State Archives, where records of the Eichmann trial are stored, there is no evidence that Gemma's memoir was used and no copy of her manuscript was found.

thausen concentration camp, told the reporter that Herman had been beaten for six weeks. Dr. Klar, a Hungarian survivor, was then living in Manhattan. Mrs. Annamarie Thiel Robertson, a Ravensbrück survivor who lived in Rego Park, Queens, told the reporter that she never failed to help observe Mrs. Gluck's birthday.

The publication of Gemma's *My Story* in the fall of 1961 resulted in several newspaper reporters coming to interview her in her low-income New York City Housing Authority apartment in Queens.[2] "Mrs. Gluck, enfeebled by the lingering effects of a stroke, lives today in Queensbridge Houses, a low-rent city project built, coincidentally, during the administration of the Little Flower," Alex Benson (1961) wrote in the *New York World-Telegram and Sun.* "Propped in an armchair with pillows, Mrs. Gluck said in an interview that she hoped her book would teach a lesson in 'humanity' and make clear that 'in every person there is something good.' "

"I want those who read my book to believe that it is a true story, no exaggeration," she told the reporter. She then commented about her famous brother: "We knew Fiorello was destined for success, even when he was a young man in Fiume. You know, I remember him now—how he used to lie in bed at night reading his college books. And Fiorello took me out to dances and parties. But if a young man showed too much interest in me he'd pull me away. 'Come on now,' he'd say. 'It's time to go. Come on now.' "

---

2. Queensbridge Houses, the largest and one of the earliest low-income housing projects in the United States, was built by the La Guardia administration in 1939. A 2005 documentary by Selena Blake, "Queensbridge: The Other Side," traces the history of the project. See Berger (2005).

Speaking to a reporter from the *New York Herald Tribune,* Gemma repeated some of the statements from her memoir: "Being a La Guardia was the reason for my incarceration in Mauthausen and in Ravensbrück, but ultimately the name La Guardia saved my life and those of my daughter and grandson. I decided that afterwards, if I survived, I wanted people to know what had happened there. So I stuck my nose all over. I saw everything and wrote it down. Even more dangerous than nosing about the camp was teaching English to other prisoners" (Stix 1961).

The article describes her housing complex, where she had then lived for fourteen years with Yolanda and grandson Richard, both of whom were also in Ravensbrück: "The elevator stops only on alternate floors. The apartment is filled with china, ornaments and photographs of her grandchildren . . . and a large and handsome photograph of her famous brother."

Gemma is portrayed as speaking "slowly and with some difficulty—she is partially paralyzed from a stroke." Although she no longer went out much, she had managed to see the Broadway play *Fiorello* and said that she loved it. She added that she was "proud of her brother and his accomplishments, but never took much interest in the political side of his career." Two neighbors took care of Gemma during the day, according to the article.

Richard was seventeen years old at the time of the article. Gemma described him as "a sweet boy who loves his grandmother," and said he wanted to go to college, even if he would have to work at the same time to pay for it. Yolanda was at the time working in the insurance department of the Amalgamated Clothing Workers Union. Gemma told the reporter that her brother had planned to buy a little house for her and her daughter and grandson and to provide for the boy's education, but he died before these ends could be accomplished. Gemma repeated to the reporter the words she had written toward the end of her memoir: "All Fiorello's plans for us vanished with his death," she said. "But at least we were in the land of opportunity, the land of the free. There was hope here."

About a year after *My Story* was published, Gemma was again mentioned in the *New York Times*. This time the headline read: "Mrs. Gluck, Sister of Ex-Mayor, Dies. Former Gemma La Guardia Was Imprisoned by Nazis." Gemma, age eighty-one, died of a heart attack on November 2, 1962, at Elmhurst General Hospital in Queens. "Mrs. Gluck was a spirited woman who often displayed flashes of the dark-eyed fire and determination that had been her brother's mien," according to the obituary. The *Times* quoted S. L. Shneiderman, who had edited Gemma's *My Story*: "She was almost a copy of her brother. Despite the suffering she had survived several strokes, she was full of energy, full of life and plans. She had a big picture of her brother in her room and she was always dreaming of his life. Recently she was writing a kind of poetry, and she was always thinking about having a volume of poetry published. She often played the violin and the piano for the children in the neighborhood" *(New York Times* 1962).

My Story was published much earlier than most memoirs that deal with the Holocaust and before interest in the subject began to escalate later in the 1960s. Gemma died only a year after the book's publication, and soon other firsthand accounts of the Holocaust began to emerge. While Gemma's memoir is much more than that, it eventually went out of print and was forgotten. Even the original publisher, David McKay Company, went out of business. Shneiderman died in October 1996.

Today most people are surprised that Fiorello had a sister in Ravensbrück, and that they had a Jewish mother. Some young people have not even heard of Gemma's famous brother, let alone Gemma. They have no idea why New York City has, among other places, an airport, a high school, and a community college named LaGuardia. Not only New York, but even Tel Aviv has a street named LaGuardia because Fiorello was considered a friend and supporter of pre-state Israel.

This new edition of Gemma's memoir makes Gemma's saga available to new generations of readers, and also makes them aware of her family history: her roots in Italy as part of the illustrious Luzzatto family, and her connection to her famous brother Fiorello, the beloved mayor of New York City from 1934 to 1945.

Gemma has been gone for almost almost half a century, but she lives on in both her memoir and her descendants. She was survived by her daughter Yolanda Denes and grandson Richard as well as her daughter Irene Roberts and Irene's three children, James, Gladys, and Clifford. Yolanda died in May 1982. Irene, who played the violin and was married to John Andrew Roberts, died on January 6, 1996. Richard Denes and his wife have four children. Richard's life has not been easy. As many Holocaust survivors, their children, and their grandchildren can testify, the damage that Hitler inflicted did not stop at the end of World War II.

Gemma's brothers, Fiorello and Richard, also had children, and now there are new generations of La Guardias. Fiorello married his first wife, Thea Almerigotti, in March 1919, and she gave birth to Fioretta Thea in June 1920. Tragically, the baby died of tuberculosis in May 1921, and six months later, at age twenty-six, Thea died of the same disease. Fiorello married

Marie Fisher, his secretary since 1916, in February 1929, and they adopted two children.

Gemma and Fiorello's brother Richard Dodge La Guardia, the youngest of the three children, was born at Fort Sully, Dakota Territories, where their father Achille was an army bandmaster. Richard became a translator for Cunard Lines. He later worked for the Y.M.C.A. and eventually settled in Trenton, New Jersey. He was educational and welfare director of the state prison in Trenton for fifteen years. He died of a heart attack in February 1935 at age forty-seven. Richard and his wife, Mary Kozar La Guardia, had three children: Richard, Jr., Irene, and Marie Gemma. Richard's son and daughters all had children, and now there are grandchildren and great-grandchildren.

Without going into details that are by now unprovable hearsay, at some point a schism developed among the branches of the La Guardia family. One person remembers that Gemma's daughter Irene was not treated well by one of her aunts. Another wonders why Gemma ended up living in a low-income public housing project. One of Gemma's great nieces mourns that she was a teenager when Gemma's original *My Story* was published in 1961 but only learned of the book recently. She had known hardly anything about her great aunt. And some people who know why there was bitterness in the family simply are not talking or do not want to be quoted.

Dredging up old family problems is pointless, especially since we can never know the full story. Instead, Gemma's story, in this new expanded edition, will end on a positive note, as she ended the original and as she would have wished. After generations of separation, this new edition of *My Story* has begun to bring the branches of the family together. Gemma's granddaughter Gladys had no idea that her great uncle Richard had granddaughters about her age, and they are now in contact and excited to have discovered each other. Fiorello's son attended a lecture related to this book in 2005 in New York City along with his daughters. Gemma's granddaughter was also present, and the family members had the opportunity to visit with each other. Gemma always had a strong sense of the importance of family, as her memoir attests. I believe she would be pleased that almost five decades after its first publication, her memoir has connected a new generation of her family.

Gemma vowed in Ravensbrück that she would tell her story so that the world could learn how she and her camp sisters suffered there. She would surely be gratified that her book is again available, and that new generations of readers can learn about her life and family, as well as her eyewitness account of the horrors of Ravensbrück and her hardships as a displaced person. Despite her terrible suffering, which she details in her memoir, she always remained optimistic and had hope for the future.

Rochelle G. Saidel

Appendix

References

Letters by or between Gemma La Guardia Gluck and Fiorello La Guardia, July 1945–May 1947

LETTER FROM GEMMA to Fiorello (her first letter), July 15, 1945, Charlottenburg, Berlin:

My dear Fiorello and Marie:

I was permitted to send you this letter, therefore, I'm writing. I wish you to know that since I spoke to you last Tuesday, I feel much better and am not worrying any more; as I know you are doing all in my behalf.

We three are feeling already much better, especially our little Richard. Of course the imprisonment handicapped him as being sixteen months old, he has not yet any teeth out, can't stand nor walk, but now we don't fear and all will be o.k. with him.

All these letters are held in the LaGuardia and Wagner Archives, LaGuardia Community College, City University of New York, New York.

Miss [Kathryn] Craven[s], the captain, is very kind to us, and she with other American officers often visit[s] us. The other day, she gave me 500 marks which she said you told her to give me.

The lady I'm living with would not hear of my paying (she's not at all interested); but I told her my brother has said I must pay and if she doesn't accept the money, I'll be compelled to go where I can pay (as I must do as my brother wishes). So finally I arranged with her to pay 5 marks a day. I have a good room, light and food. I think this is quite reasonable, don't you? Of course we have the most simple food (as there's no food to be bought here). So this will be about 150–155 marks a month.

Today, Mr. [Frederick] Carroll from American Red Cross of Paris came with your cable. I read it. O, Fiorello, you're a dear fellow, to see how you are working for us—keep it up, try to find our husbands and get us soon over to U.S.A. (but I should like to come with a ship and not with an air-plane [*sic*] as I fear my heart is too weak and I think a sea-voyage would do me good).

Mr. Carroll asked how much money I wanted. I told him that I got through Miss Cravens from you already a sum and just now, I have not much use as we can't buy anything (perhaps later the shops will open). As there's a great scarcity of food, Mr. Carroll said he's going to speak with the Americans to provide me with food (especially for Richard).

Miss Cravens and the Americans are very kind and nice to us, of course on account of you, "Little Flower" (they told me you are so called now).

Please F. try to search for our husbands if they are

alive, if in B[uda]pest or where they are. *Notes:* Herman Gluck born in Mako Hungary on August 6th 1881, residing in B[uda]pest. Correspondent in Credit Bank, arrested in our home on June 7th 1944, he and I were brought to *Mauthausen* bei Linz (Austria) cell 26. I left him there on June 19th 1944 (since then don't know *anything from him*).

Erno Denes (my son-in-law, born in Vienna, on April 7th 1887), Hungarian citizen, merchant, arrested on August 1st, 1944 from our home, Nagymezo utca 43, 11, 5 brought to *Buda prison* in Gyorskocsi utca, from there is unknown which camp he's been brought to. Please try to find out. From here we are also trying to make searches.

My six room apartment in B[uda]pest is said to be destroyed and all stolen, so we have absolutely nothing—but I don't care if we are all alive.

I don't want to write about what we went through, this I shall tell you all when we shall be together. Of course dear F. I hope it's understood that our husbands are also going to be brought over. I sent a snapshot with Dr. Carroll made by the American boys. The lady holding Richard is Capt. Cravens. Richard is a real sweet and good baby. He was the one who kept us alive, as I can assure you in one year's imprisonment one got such moments where one lost courage and the thoughts of that baby kept up my spirit.

Now Fiorello, you worried me, by not saying anything about my Irene [Gemma's daughter, who immigrated to the United States from Budapest in 1938]. Is she well? Healthy? What is she doing? Do write and let one know. You can understand that I am anxious to know all about her.

I'm glad to hear that the American Red Cross is going to be already in Berlin.

The family I'm living with are simple people, employees and antifacista family, not at all interested. Where we live we are in the English Zone and we are all protected.

Please now don't worry, we are all improving and since I heard your voice, am no more ill and not worrying. Please keep me informed and tell me always what I am to do and get us over as soon as possible and find our husbands. Let Irene know of this letter, give her my love and kisses.

Love and kisses for your dear self, Marie and children. Yolanda sends her love and Richard sends a kiss.

Your sister Gemma

Letter from Gemma to Fiorello, September 11, 1945, Charlottenburg, Berlin:

My dear Fiorello and Marie:

A certain Mr. [Daniel] De Luce, from the "Associated Press" comes every now and then, to visit us, see how we are, if we need something and if I wish to write. Today, for the first time I took occasion of this opportunity and send you this letter, begging you to give me soon an answer. In the first place, I must tell you, it's, for Yolanda and me, a great pleasure and good feeling to see the great interest you are taking in our behalf. I was called to visit Major Novak, your friend, who was very kind to us. He told us that you are making all steps to search for our husbands; that now the Americans are in Austria and things can go on quicker; he stated about Gen. Clark, the commander in Vienna, who is your friend, that he will visit him personally and speak all about us. Here the Broadcasting Company has also called Vienna and Budapest searching our husbands but until now no results. Then Mr. Novak said that you can get us out either in Cuba or Canada—Look here Fiorello, I'm *too* feeble and exhausted to make plans or decisions, I leave all in your hands, I know you will guide us in the best way. Only this I *do* wish to state, we should like to *get out* of Berlin, before winter sets in; there is a great scarcity of food, no coal etc. before us for the winter season. Then although in winter the climate of Cuba is preferable, still we should like better *to come to Canada,* which is much nearer to N.Y. and I would be quieter to know that in Canada you all are in my vicinity. How long should we have to remain here? The Americans advise us to get out of Berlin. An officer came in the name of Mr. Carroll of the American Red Cross in Paris to visit us last week. He also stated that the Americans being in Vienna will be able to procure some news from Mauthausen by Linz, and perhaps also from Budapest. Mr. Carroll is working in every way making searches, he is also in connection with Gen. Clark, and has notified the [International] Red Cross.

God grant that a good result will come from this researching, Fiorello dear! I'm not complaining, but you do understand me don't you? When I tell you that when I was imprisoned and had to resign myself to *their* will and was not free to speak or act; I was not so unhappy as I am now. We are five months already in Berlin, unable to do anything—no signs of our husbands—with the thoughts of knowing that we have *no* more home—no *clothes—no papers, no position.* We are like beggars—and if it wouldn't be *for you,* perhaps nobody would take notice of us and in that case without money we could also starve here. But being your sister the Americans are very kind to me and through you the U.S.A. Red Cross are providing baby with food—also here the head lady of the "Anti-Faschismus Society," who was also in Ravensbrück Camp, we knew each other there and she is very very kind to us. Of course Yolanda, little Richard and I are all three victims of the Faschismus and belong to this Society. You must know Fiorello dear, that all the time of my imprisonment, you had no reason to be ashamed of me. I held my head always proudly up, was full of energy—hopes and faith; but now come such moments (Yolanda shouldn't know of this) that I'm losing all my hopes and am beginning to *fear* that perhaps our Herman and Erno are not living and if this should be the case then Fiorello dear, *as soon as* you *can take* us *away* from here, let us at least be near you and my Irene as our lives will be unbearable.

Now Fiorello, I should like to ask you a couple of questions—*first* should I go (before coming to America) to Budapest to see if something from our belongings is still existing? It takes about ten days to get there and being weak I confess I *fear* to travel *alone* there especially as I also have a feeling that all our things are *lost*. *Second*. When do you think of getting us out—if before winter all is well—but if after winter then we shall have to procure *warm clothing* for all three of us! as we only have the clothes which are on our backs and these dresses are not adapted for winter; and then I also am afraid to travel in winter with little Richard. Remember I don't want to change your plans; but I must know to be able to direct myself and for *different reasons* I do think it would *be advisable* to get us over before winter sets in.

Here one is teasing me to take a small flat if I stop here in winter and for this I also want *your* advice. The family where I live *cannot* be kinder or more attentive to us, and I like to be with them as I feel more assured to live near someone than to be quite alone. Then as I'm living now, it's not costing so much and taking a small flat which would cost at least R.M. 120 monthly with other extra expenses—light, etc. would make it much more expensive and this I don't want you to spend superfluous money for us: But the head-lady of the Anti-Faschismus Society is also *right*—she says "if you are living alone the Americans will perhaps provide you with coal—the Red Cross brings food for baby and perhaps also for you" (now you'll understand living here—I can't eat alone and let them look at us eating—so that now and then I give them also something) and in winter where everybody knows that the scarcity of food will be great and that one must save *every little bit*—one advises me to live on *my own* so this problem you must also *absolve* [*sic*] for me.

For me it's a terrible feeling that you must spend so

much for me; but what can we do? Here in Berlin we are helpless—all has been stolen from us. And if Herman would be near me, he could help us—but for the present moment I have only *you*, Fiorello. You will know that all the victims of the Faschismus when returning to their countries are recompensed, getting back all (many more) than they have lost—homes, furniture—money, clothes, positions, shops, etc. If I would have gone back to Budapest—Yolanda and I as well as our husbands could have demanded this and I'm sure they would have *richly recompensed* us. Also, here in Berlin, I could get a cottage or a home, a position, *anything* I want (not on your account as all the victims are receiving these recompensations); but here I assure you on *your account* I *don't accept* anything. I only take from the American Red Cross as I know Mr. Carroll told me it comes *through you.*

Please write something about my Irene. Is she healthy? Married? Or is she working? I'm anxious to hear all you know about her. Does she know that we were all imprisoned? And that we three are alive? O Fiorello bring us soon together. I am going on my 65th birthday and really this was not a bodily but a great soul suffering and I am a victim of this blow, and suffered to see the others suffer; I'll tell you all when we shall be together—I've written much down—I want America to *know* and not to *forget* the cruelties of these beasts.

Last week, I felt so bad that I had to put myself in the hands of a doctor—blood pressure 240 and heart very weak. I weigh now 104 pounds; when I went to the camp [I] weighed 150. I had to change my eye-glasses for 1/2 number stronger. Yolanda had to go to be treated by a dentist (as to keep her child alive she nursed him till he was 14 months old) and this destroyed her teeth, this also we must know if we stay here in winter, she'll have a complete work done; but if you'll call us away *before* (which I hope you will) then she'll make only the most necessary work, the rest in U.S.A. So dear Fiorello for the doctor, dentist and if we must buy some warm clothes we shall need money—I don't want to ask the Red Cross. Please you arrange it. For living I have still for a couple of months. Don't be angry that I speak so openly to you but *you are all* that I have today. You'll see when Herman will be near me, he'll work again, he's intelligent and so *so diligent*. Please write immediately to us and continue to search for my dear husband and son-in-law. Fiorello dear, we have no papers; if you need for traveling here are some important dates.

Best love from Yolanda, Richard and I for You, Marie, and my Irene.

With many kisses. Your Gemma . . .

Special love and kisses for [Fiorello's children and] Mary from Trenton [widow of Gemma and Fiorello's brother Richard] with children—I'll be so happy to be with you all and Fiorello dear, knowing *your* love for children, I'm sure you'll love *our* little Richard (perhaps you'll have to be a father to him).

❧

First letter from Fiorello to Gemma, October 31, 1945, New York, N.Y.:

Dear Gemma,

This is the first opportunity I have had to get a letter to you through proper legal channels. The regular mail is not yet opened from the U.S. to Germany, hence I could not write to you and I would not do anything to violate the law. I have been in constant touch and am informed concerning you and the conditions under which you are living. The Red Cross has been very good and very kind.

Because of the limitation of space in this letter, I will get right down to the point. I need not tell you of my anxiety for your welfare. You know that. Your situation is extremely difficult. No exceptions can be made. If any different treatment were applied to you, it would cause hundreds of thousands of demands for the same treatment. The publicity which you obtained and the fact that I might be known, makes it all the more difficult. But let me repeat, your case is the same as that of hundreds of thousands of displaced people.

I will provide for you and do the very best that conditions will permit. You must be patient. People have been very kind to you. I am thankful for it. I think you displayed a little impatience in your letter to Mr. Carroll. By the way, he was killed in an automobile accident a few days ago.

You have lost your citizenship, therefore that is something that cannot be remedied. Notwithstanding, out of kindliness, help has been given to you and will continue to be given to you.

I had a talk with Mr. Harvey Gibson [president of Manufacturers Trust Company and a Red Cross commissioner], who is a friend of mine, only yesterday. I understand you received $100 from the Red Cross and then again $100. I have reimbursed the Red Cross. I have not yet reimbursed the $50 which you received from Miss Cravens, but will do so as soon as I can see her.

I learn with a great deal of disappointment that displaced nationals in Germany cannot be sent anywhere. I am trying my best to have you sent either to Sweden or England or Portugal or Italy. There are many insurmountable obstacles. Again, if they do it for one they will have to do it for hundreds of thousands. I will try my best. I will then be able to provide for you and you can get an apartment, and of course, living conditions will be so much better.

As to your returning to the United States, I am doing all I can, but I cannot get Yolanda and her child in. You do not want to leave them alone. Unless the law changes, this may continue for sometime [*sic*]. If it can be done, it will be done.

We might as well be realistic and recognize that through all the publicity which has been given to your case, that if Herman and Yolanda's husband were alive, some communication would have reached you. However, there is always hope until definite information is received.

I know of how terrible the conditions are in Germany. Therefore, I will do all I can to get you out, but please understand that if it cannot be done, we must simply reconcile ourselves to it. Then I will do the best that conditions permit to provide for you. We cannot send American currency or packages to Germany now. As soon as that is permitted, I will send you regular packages and money.

If the Red Cross gives me the courtesy of writing again, I will do so. You can communicate with me in like manner.

You have been through so much. I know you will have the good sense to manage for a short time until something can be done. Be very careful in the statements that you make.

With love and hoping for the best I am
Sincerely yours, Fiorello

Fiorello wrote that this letter was supposed to be sent to Gemma via the Red Cross, and she mentions in chapter 19 of *My Story* that she received her first letter from Fiorello in fall 1945. From correspondence in December 1945 it is clear that Fiorello was then having trouble sending mail to Gemma. He received a letter, dated December 29, 1945, from Acting Adjutant General Edward F. Witsell of the War Department, about problems and regulations regarding postal service to Berlin.

Fiorello then went right to the top to get his correspondence through to Gemma. He also made a more consequential request.

❦

Letter from Fiorello La Guardia to General Dwight D. Eisenhower, January 7, 1946, New York, N.Y.:

My dear General:

I have found some difficulty in getting a letter to my sister. If no violation of rules is involved, I would greatly appreciate it if the enclosed could be delivered to her. Of course, you are free to open same. I can assure you that there is no violation of any existing rules in the contents.

I received word from the Danish Minister that arrangements have been made for Gemma's entrance into Denmark. I am very grateful for this. However, if it is possible to get her into the Italian Section of Switzerland or into any English speaking country, it would be much better because of language.

Thanking you for your courtesy.

Letter from Fiorello to Gemma, December 4, 1946, New York, N.Y.:

Dear Gemma:

It is so difficult to ship anything that I thought you could make better use of money. I also thought that you would want to make some little gifts around the house to the people who have been good to you and I am therefore sending you a draft for $35—$25 for your Christmas and $10 for gifts to those who have helped to make you comfortable. I am sending this in the same manner as I send your usual remittance. I hope you are all well.

With love,

❧

Letter from Gemma to Fiorello, April 2, 1947, Hellerup, Denmark:

My Dear Ones:

In haste I write this good news—Yolanda has received her "Quota No. 801–802" and I must say the legation here is working in great tempo—they called Yolanda down immediately and said one must do all quickly one thing after the other—Well, it was necessary for her to get a paper from the Denmark Police that she's not been punished, *this she got* then have a passport picture with Richard taken *this is done* then to bring all at the Central Police and immediately she got a "Provisory Passport" as there is no Hungarian Consul, she couldn't get a Hungarian passport—a Danish one she can't get so this is the way she was immediately helped, this Provisory Passport is sufficient for her departure it's valid till *June 1st 1947* (if we are not off till then) one will prolong it. We received our permit to stay still 3 months in Copenhagen valid till *July 1st 1947* but this I believe we don't get anymore.

Now the Consul at the legation congratulated Yolly [how] quickly all went and they are finished now, he said. Your uncle must do the rest to procure the steamer's tickets and if he wishes we are at his disposal to help also in this line, but he thinks it's much easier from America and he gave Yolanda a list of ships to mention them to you. And he doesn't advise to travel to England, it makes the trip much more expensive and [illegible] knows with baby it wouldn't be fun. Here from Copenhagen are ships—freight ships of American Line the best of these is McCormick and it's best to book from N.Y. These ships take only 12 passengers and takes naturally a longer time, they are also very clean; then once a month, May 6, June 6th, or July 5 comes a big Polish ship the Batony to Copenhagen one says this would be very good. Then from Sweden are leaving every fortnight a ship so I leave this to you only notify us in time what you have decided and the legation also wants to know if they are to book tickets for us or if you are doing so. Now Fiorello, if you have deposited money for these expenses, why did they make *me* pay? Today they told Yolanda they think some money is deposited. That time they said they couldn't cash it, that I must pay. I did so and I owe that C. 180 to Mrs. Nimb, so please if the money is there authorize them to give me that money as I want to pay Mrs. Nimb. I have been 12 days ill in bed with muscular rheumatism. I called the doctor once C. 10. medicine C.5 if I have to have 15 days massage at 3 cronies a day as here lives in the pension a lady who gives massages. Otherwise it would cost 5 cronies each time. I was so angry as in the camp I wasn't ill and here the whole winter I was o.k. And as spring comes I get ill. I'm up now, I must get in order to travel. Please Fiorello dear write all clearly now and when we shall travel and give us *all directions*. Also, let me know what am I to do about Richard? Shall I take him to a Psycho-Analyst [*sic*]? Perhaps it is safer to have a paper in our hands. The doctor here when he came to me, I asked him, he said, the child has developed very well and he is alright but if *you* wish it, to do it, he'll give me a good address. But I suppose this will be expensive, I have no idea. Please answer me also in this subject. For clothes you must not worry for spring and summer now we can pull through. I should like to buy for Richard a pair of shoes—some socks, 1 or 2 little blouses. What am I to do with the "Radio?" I can get from a lady here in the pension C. 100 for it. So please advise. I am so happy to think soon we shall be in N.Y. And near you all. . . . It'll be just wonderful and perhaps in this atmosphere some things we'll be able to forget.

Please answer soon. The Consul advised Yolanda to address your letter so as if you are not there, it won't delay as Marie can open your letter and inform you. Best love from us all. Yolanda [and] baby are also so happy to think we are going soon.

Kisses, Gemma

Letter from Fiorello to Gemma, April 19, 1947, New York, N.Y.:

Dear Gemma:

This is to advise you that I have made arrangements with the Moore-McCormack Lines for your passage. In all likelihood it will be either in June or July. You will board the ship in Copenhagen. The agents of the steamship will get in touch with you through the American Legation. I will pay the passage from this end.

Now this is a very simple matter. Do not complicate

it or involve it with a lot of talk. When you are called, all you will have to do is to show your documents, get your steamship tickets, and when you get the steamship tickets you have nothing else to do but get on the ship the day it sails. Do not show off during the passage.

I am sure you will find the ship most comfortable. I will keep you advised.

Your birthday is on the 24th and we all send you our best wishes for many happy returns.

Affectionately,

References

Archival Sources

All text citations to the following sources use the abbreviations preceding the names of the archives.

LBI   Leo Baeck Institute Archive, New York, N.Y.

LGW   LaGuardia and Wagner Archives, LaGuardia Community College, City University of New York, New York, N.Y.

MGR   Archive of Mahn- und Gedenkstätte Ravensbrück, Stiftung Brandenburgische Gedenkstätten, Fürstenberg, Germany

SLS   S. L. Shneiderman Archives, Diaspora Research Institute, Tel Aviv University, Ramat Aviv, Israel

YV   Archive Collection of Yad Vashem, Jerusalem, Israel

All Other Sources

Anthonioz, Genevieve De Gaulle. 1999. *The Dawn of Hope: A Memoir of Ravensbrück*. New York: Arcade.

Benson, Alex. 1961. " 'My Story' Is One of Humanity: La Guardia Sister Tells of Nazi Camp Days." *New York World-Telegram and Sun*, 25 October. Copy in SLS.

Berger, Joseph. 2005. "Her Film Project Happens to Be Her Project." *New York Times*, 14 December.

Braham, Randolph. 2000. *The Politics of Genocide: The Holocaust in Hungary.* Detroit: Wayne State University Press.

Brodsky, Alyn. 2003. *The Great Mayor.* New York: St. Martin's Press.

Hilberg, Raul. 1985. *The Destruction of the European Jews.* New York: Holmes and Meier.

New York Times. 1961. "La Guardia's Sister Marks 80th Year: Memory of Nazi Camp Mars Party for Mrs. Gluck." 23 April, p. 38. Copy in SLS.

————. 1962. "Mrs. Gluck, Sister of Ex-Mayor, Dies; Former Gemma La Guardia Was Imprisoned by Nazis." 3 November. Copy in SLS.

Póltawska, Wanda. 1964. *And I Am Afraid of My Dreams.* New York: Hippocrene Books.

Rossiter, Margaret. 1986. *Women in the Resistance.* New York: Praeger.

Saidel, Rochelle. 2004. *The Jewish Women of Ravensbrück Concentration Camp.* Madison: University of Wisconsin Press.

Silbermann, Lotte. 2000. "In der SS-Kantine in Ravensbrück." In *Frauen-KZ Ravensbrück,* ed. Helga Schwarz and Gerda Szepansky, 59. Potsdam: Brandenburgischen Landeszentrale für politische Bildung.

Stix, Harriet. 1961. "La Guardia's Sister Publishes Her Story." *New York Herald Tribune,* 26 October. Copy in SLS.

Symonowicz, Wanda, ed. 1970. *Beyond Human Endurance: The Ravensbrück Women Tell Their Stories.* Warsaw: Interpress Publishers.

Trenton Evening Times. 1935. "LaGuardia Burial Will Be Saturday," 7 February.

A Woman in Berlin: Eight Weeks in the Conquered City. 2005. New York: Henry Holt.

Yehil, Leni. 1990. *The Holocaust: The Fate of European Jewry.* New York: Oxford University Press.